# Justice

## Islamic and Western Perspectives

# Justice

## Islamic and Western Perspectives

Zafar Iqbal

THE ISLAMIC FOUNDATION

*Published by*

THE ISLAMIC FOUNDATION

Markfield Conference Centre, Ratby Lane,
Markfield, Leicestershire, LE67 9SY, UK
Tel: 01530-244944, Fax: 01530-244946
E-mail: i.foundation@islamic-foundation.org.uk
http//www.islamic-foundation.org.uk

Quran House, P.O. Box 30611, Nairobi, Kenya

PMB 3196, Kano, Nigeria

Copyright © Islamic Foundation, 2007/1428 AH

All rights reserved. No part of this publication may be reproduced, stored in
a retrieval system, or transmitted in any form or by any means, electronic,
mechanical, photocopying, recording, or otherwise, without the prior
permission of the copyright owner.

*British Library Cataloguing-in-Publication Data*
A catalogue record for this book is available from the British Library

ISBN 10: 0–86037–590–0
ISBN 13: 978-0–86037–590–6

Printed and bound in Great Britain by
Antony Rowe Ltd, Chippenham, Wiltshire

Typeset by: N.A. Qaddoura
Cover design: Nasir Cadir

# Contents

# Transliteration Table

*Arabic Consonants*

Initial, unexpressed medial and final:

| | | | | | | | |
|---|---|---|---|---|---|---|---|
| ء | ' | د | d | ض | ḍ | ك | k |
| ب | b | ذ | dh | ط | ṭ | ل | l |
| ت | t | ر | r | ظ | ẓ | م | m |
| ث | th | ز | z | ع | ' | ن | n |
| ج | j | س | s | غ | gh | هـ | h |
| ح | ḥ | ش | sh | ف | f | و | w |
| خ | kh | ص | ṣ | ق | q | ي | y |

*Vowels, diphthongs, etc.*

Short:  ﹷ a   ﹻ i   ﹹ u

Long:  ﺎﹷ ā   ﹻﻲ ī   ﻮﹹ ū

Diphthongs:  ﻮﹷ aw

ﻰﹷ ay

# Foreword

*O you who believe! Stand out firmly for justice, as witnesses to Allah, even as against yourselves, or your parents, or your kin, and whether it be (against) rich or poor: for Allah can best protect both. Follow not the lusts (of your hearts), lest you swerve, and if you distort (justice) or decline to do justice, verily Allah is well-acquainted with all that you do.* (Qur'ān 4:135)

This book is about justice. It is about the blueprint of a social order aimed at restoring equilibrium, harmony and peace. Historically, two schools of thought have illuminated this inquiry: the religious school and the secular school. In this title, the religious school is epitomized by Islam while the secular school is represented by a range of select ancient and contemporary views on justice considered most influential in setting the direction of intellectual debate on this subject. The promise that both these schools offer to their adherents revolves around answering the intriguing question of what constitutes good life. Islam seeks to address this inquiry by taking the position that life is the creation of Allah Who has created humankind to serve as His vicegerent on the earth. In this capacity, people are required to acknowledge Allah, worship Him alone, and manage affairs of the world and use its resources in accordance with His revealed will in the Holy Qur'ān and the *Sunnah* of the Prophet (peace be upon him). In submitting to this Will lies the secret of good life according to the teachings of Islam. Revelation in this paradigm, therefore, is not only a manual of instruction on faith (*'aqīdah*), worship (*'ibādah*), and individual morality (*khulq*) but also a source of general principles of socio-economic and legal guidance which elaborate the concept of justice for social organization.

The religious understanding on life and its purpose has attracted fierce criticism from the secular schools since olden times. It is argued that principles of ethics, economics and politics do not need the aid of metaphysics and can be rationally extracted by reflecting on the life of human beings in a social setting. However, in the absence of a purpose established for mankind from outside, existence understandably becomes an aimless and brute 'absurdity' in the secular theory. In a bid to provide life some meaning through philosophical speculation, the focus is shifted to a number of options including Aristotelian stress on virtue, Kantian emphasis on obligation, and the nineteenth and twentieth century philosophers' accent on preference satisfaction. These reflections, severely at odds with one another, as they cannot but be, work as building blocks of a secular social order and remain infested with contradictions or tensions. The author has done a good job in bypassing the heuristics used in deriving such perspectives and focused instead on the crux of the matter, i.e. the principles advanced for political, economic, and social organization in such thought-streams. Once these diverse principles are critically examined, a comparison between the religious and the secular views sets the scene for an objective assessment of the Islamic position. This evaluation indeed provides a fitting climax to the author's insightful, penetrating, and at times, breathtaking argument on the pros and cons of many competing perspectives on justice.

There are a number of ways in which this monograph is expected to make a contribution to the existing literature on justice. First, it is a timely effort in examining the substance of contemporary theories on justice from the vantage point of Islam. Such an endeavour had become overdue after a renewed interest in moral philosophy in the Western tradition since the appearance of *A Theory of Justice* by John Rawls in 1971. Second, this attempt opens up the possibilities for a rational dialogue between Islam and the West on issues widely acknowledged as the root cause of discord between the two civilizations, in fact of the underlying currents of contemporary civilizational crisis. In doing so, it provides an opportunity for readers to rise above the stereotypical images of Islam and evaluate it on logical terms *pari passu* with the contemporary Western philosophies. Third, this study provides an occasion to appreciate and celebrate the common concerns of humanity as elucidated in threads that run across a range of humanistic Western perspectives on justice and Islam. In fact, it is very clear from the research presented that the differences of opinion among multiple secular positions are starker than those between them and Islam. As the author argues, the Islamic position lies somewhere in the middle of a range of secular liberalisms and Marxian perspectives. Fourth, it is important to reflect deeply on the differences between the Western and the Islamic perspectives, too. In my view, some of these differences stem from an *ad hoc* and inherently fragmented approach to knowledge and society imbued in the conventional social science approach. As 'empirical' evidence grows on the connection between human actions on the one hand and social disruption and environmental disasters on the other, humanity is compelled to belatedly admit its bounded rationality.

At this critical juncture, Islam can play a role in holding the hands of the 'rational animal' and connect him back with the Superior Intellect without Whose Guidance the human mind cannot transcend oneself and rise above the compulsions and attractions of 'here and now' in order to reconcile self-interest with communal harmony and values of justice, freedom and world peace.

In the end, I hope this study will be of interest to students and scholars of diverse interests including those focusing on Islamic economics, political philosophy and global social movements. Equally, I hope it stimulates a series of attempts to provide a more expanded version of Islamic principles of economic and political justice to serve the dual purpose of developing a characteristically Islamic alternative to modernity and participating fully in the global inter-civilizational dialogue on the future shape of the world.

Leicester                                          **Khurshid Ahmad**
December 14, 2006
Dhu'l-Qaʿdah 23, 1427 AH

# *Introduction*

Humanity is in a state of confusion. It is torn apart by conflicting claims of civilizational superiority. In the twentieth century alone, the rival views on how society should organize itself have been contested, in the words of Stiglitz (1994, p.1), not just in the debating halls of academe but on the battlefields of (Europe, Japan,) Korea, Vietnam, Afghanistan, and Central America. And, as this conflict reaches the Middle East and Central Asia, the focus has shifted increasingly to the weakest link in the chain, i.e. Islam. Contemporary Islam is under attack from all directions. Its claim of furnishing a blueprint for an egalitarian social order has turned it into a villain of a host of competing secular and religious interests. Its unfailing capacity to stir the hearts and minds of people has facilitated its association with terrorism. And, its hold on lands rich in natural resources has made it a prime target of those perpetually unsatiated with over consumption.

The question arises, therefore, as to how Muslims ought to respond to these challenges? How should they positively engage with this worldwide Hobbesian struggle for political, social, economic and military control? One possible answer lies in Muslims clarifying and justifying their vision of a social order in a language understandable to modernity. For, to the extent that misunderstandings lie at the core of the East-West relationship, clarification of ideas can play a pivotal role in alleviating hostilities and providing a focal point for intellectual debate and dialogue among civilizations.

This monograph has been written precisely with this objective in mind. It brings together and integrates key elements of Islam on organizing various dimensions of a good society. This synthesis is undertaken against the backdrop of different philosophical traditions that have influenced the contemporary Western concept of political order. The idea of justice on which, to the joy of Islam, Western moral philosophy has dwelled over the past four decades to articulate its position(s) on this issue, provides the common thread around which this entire study is formulated.

# *Justice:*
## *Islamic and Western Perspectives*

**WHAT IS JUSTICE?**

The idea that a society should organize itself on principles of justice and that government ought to play a primary role in securing such justice is well known in history. In the fifth century CE, St. Augustine remarked: *'Remota justitia, quid sint regna nisi magna latrocinia'* (Removed from justice, what be rulers if not large-scale robbers?). But, what is justice? According to Miller (1991, p.260), the best general definition comes from the Byzantine emperor, Justinian (482-565 CE): justice is the constant and perpetual will to render to everyone his due. One aspect of justice, called distributive justice, attempts to elaborate 'what it means to give people what is due to them' by identifying a morally correct principle that connects the characteristics of people with their rights and obligations. Some principles that can serve this purpose are listed in Table 1.1 below.

### Table 1.1: Alternative principles of justice

| | |
|---|---|
| • To each according to merit | • To each according to need |
| • To each according to individual effort | • To each according to societal contribution |
| • To each according to rights | • To each an equal share |

Based on Beauchamp and Bowie (2001, p.642).

A theory of justice might accept only one, more, or all of these principles as legitimate (Beauchamp and Bowie, 2001). Sen (1992, pp.73-75) refers the characteristics across which a theory of justice establishes – explicitly or implicitly – a 'basal equality' amongst human beings as the substantive content or the informational basis of a theory of justice. But as he argues, focus on this basis alone is insufficient to comprehend the demands of justice. What matters also is the information that is excluded from a view of justice and which does not have a direct bearing on assessing alternative social arrangements and policies. It is this perspective that we shall keep in mind while examining different theories of justice advanced since the ancient Greeks.

## PRE-MODERN THOUGHT

### Greek thought

Plato (427-347 BC) and Aristotle (384-322 BC) were the first systematic political theorists of the Greek era. Plato in his *Republic*, the prototype of all utopias, considers that most people do not possess the intellect to conduct their affairs properly and need to be told what is good for them. Nevertheless, human beings are essentially social beings who find a natural fulfillment in political association. These premises lead Plato to conceive of an absolutist state that is led by a philosopher king or knowledgeable elite whose impartiality and commitment to Plato's ideals is secured through grooming, renunciation of family life and affections, as well as, abdication of private property. Such an elite would strive to actualize the moral perfection of citizens by the development of private and public virtue. The concept of individual freedom, as we are aware of it today, does not find its way into Plato's model of societal organization and if that contradicts with human nature, Plato is deliberately indifferent to it (Bowle, 1961, pp.40-42; Harmon, 1964, pp.29-52).

To Aristotle, Plato's student, the search begins with the concept of 'good'. Good is the goal, purpose, or aim to which something or somebody moves. And insofar as human beings are concerned, their good relates to their nature. Two basic aspects of the latter are humankind's political nature and their ability to speak and reason (practical rationality). The former moves them to the formation of families, clans, and ultimately, political communities. The goal is to provide necessary economic, social, and legal conditions to pursue a good life in two directions: downwards to obtain the necessities of life and upwards to achieve self-realization. Rationality, the second aspect of human nature, is comprised of different stages: thus, there is a basic sensation of pain and pleasure (raw instincts or passions) shared with animals that guides human action. And then there is a unique ability to look beyond the here and now and determine at one level what is useful and harmful and at a higher plane, what is good and bad, and just and unjust for the interests of the community as a whole. It is the latter ability that corresponds with the essential nature or *telos* of humankind and equates with moral rationality (Hoffe, 1995).

Moral rationality, thus understood, provides a link back to the political nature of humankind and the demand that they realize their *telos* by acting in accordance with justice, whereas justice is that state of character that disposes one to act fairly in dealings with other people. Seen from this angle, justice also embodies virtue, rather the whole of virtue since most moral virtues, in their essence, are social and political attitudes. However, there is a connotation in which justice may also be considered as a part of virtue. In this context it is to be considered as equality apart from any other considerations that matter. To elaborate:

> since the equal is a mean, the just will be a sort of mean too. ...
> (1) as a mean it implies two extremes, the more and the less,

(2) as equal it implies two equal shares, and (3) as just it implies certain persons for whom it is just. Consequently, justice involves at least four terms, two persons for whom it is just and two shares which are just. And there will be the same equality between the shares as between the persons, that is, the ratio between the shares will be the same as the ratio between the persons. If the persons are not equal, they will not have equal shares; it is when equals possess or are assigned unequal shares, or persons who are not equal are given equal shares, that quarrels and complaints arise. (The Nature of Justice, 1992, p.211)

Justice so equated with 'equality' is then divided further into three branches: distributive justice is concerned with the distribution of honour or money or the other divisible assets of the community (social benefits and burdens) among its members; justice in exchange stands for equality between whatever goods are exchanged and corrective justice means establishing equality between punishment and the crime.

Having clarified the scope of justice, Aristotle then integrates it with the role of the legislature and law making leading ultimately to the very important conclusion that the ruler and the elite are also subordinated to such impersonal rules/constitutions since these rules are oriented towards universal welfare. However, although the elite are subjected to such rules, a hierarchical social structure is envisaged. Citizenship is reserved only for those who are economically self-sufficient. Slaves, craftsmen, and traders are excluded. There is little room for pursuing commerce and wealth for its own sake; and trading and usury are considered as posing a threat to a person's moral well being. The government is the highest form of community employed in the struggle to attain the highest form of moral good. Thus individuals are subordinated to the state and the state to an ethical purpose (Bowle, 1961, pp.40-42; Harmon, 1964, pp.29-52; Muller, 1993, p.41).

For Aristotle himself and a small class of leisurely elite – who can afford that degree of disengagement from the necessities of life – there is a 'good' even superior to exercizing virtue in a political community. And the way to discover that good is to reflect on what is best in human beings. As we saw above, what is best in human beings is reason and one characteristic of reason is to contemplate the unchanging and timeless truths that are equated with the divine in Greek thought. It is such contemplation done as an end in itself rather than as a means to something else that constitutes the highest form of human good (MacIntyre, 1966, pp.82-3). Taken to its logical conclusion, this attitude, carries within it, the seeds of asceticism and renunciation providing reason for the elite to withdraw from active politics and pave the way for something larger than *'polis'*, an absolutist state, the then state of Macedon. As Kelson (MacIntyre, 1966) puts it:

> the glorification of the contemplative life, which has renounced all activity and more especially all political activity, has at all times constituted a typical element of the political morality set up by the ideologies of absolute monarchy. For the essential tendency of this form of state consists in excluding the subjects from all share in public affairs. (p.99)

### The Christian view

The pursuit of the spiritual and renunciation of the material reached its zenith in the teachings of Jesus Christ (pbuh). According to one view, he had little interest in politics and no qualms with the public order established by the Roman authorities. Instead, he was interested in saving souls, this by providing a corrective for Pharisaic morality. And, that too, for a short interim period, until God's Messianic kingdom arrived. Under these circumstances, as MacIntyre (1966) explains:

the only form of prudence is to look to the kingdom. To take thought of for the morrow, to lay up treasure on earth, not to sell all you have and give to the poor – these are essentially imprudent policies. You will lose your soul if you pursue such policies, precisely because the world you gain is not going to last. ... the crucial fact is that the Messianic kingdom did not come, and ... therefore the church ever since has been preaching an ethics which could not find application in a world where history had not come to an end. ... It is therefore not surprising that insofar as Christianity has propounded moral beliefs and elaborated moral concepts for ordinary human life, it has been content to accept conceptual frameworks from elsewhere. (p.116)

This mindset became evident after the Roman emperor, Constantine, embraced Christianity in the early fourth century. In the event, the passive relationship between the Church and the State, that to some was implied in the early teachings of Jesus Christ (pbuh) was set aside. Thus, St. Augustine (355-430 CE) wrote in *The City of God* that the State was a divinely ordained remedial authority over which men had no control. And as regards its aims, it was to purge men of the misery of unregulated life: greedy egotism, selfishness and slavery of lust that was the result of man being born sinful. In fact, the Church was conceived as a partner to the State in the mission of cleansing men. The theory, expressed more succinctly by Pope Gelasius I in the late fifth century, became known as the 'doctrine of the two swords' (Harmon, 1964, pp.98-131; Kramnick, 1969, pp.83-84; Bowle, 1961, p.135).

This rather hostile view of the world influenced Western thought for some eight centuries until St. Thomas Aquinas (1225-1274 CE), impressed by Aristotelian thought translated and expounded by Jewish and Muslim writers, presented the idea of a fundamental harmony between human and religious values, between the natural and the revealed law, and between reason and faith. Thus authority and socio-political institutions were necessitated not necessarily because of man's inherent sinfulness, which nevertheless remained a core belief, but instead because of the positive value they offered in arranging human affairs in accordance with the requirements of human sociable nature. The Christian concept of humankind and society, however similar in form to the Greek, nevertheless, had important differences in terms of content. Thus the list of virtues is taken from the teachings of Jesus Christ (pbuh) rather than from Aristotle (Harmon, 1964, pp.123-131; MacIntyre, 1966).

In general, until the Middle Ages, Christian thought primarily focused on presenting life as the preparatory ground for salvation. The Church had the sole and infallible authority to interpret the demands of such salvation. And these demands usually called for caring, loving, and sharing with co-religionists. It was believed that each person had a divinely ordained place in life to which he exhibited loyalty by conducting a specific (mostly hereditary) function and becoming a member of the relevant organized (occupational) group.[1] The objective was to join a moral struggle for securing the necessities of life, i.e. food, clothing and shelter. The profit motive and pursuit of wealth for its own sake were considered as sinful. As a result, trade and commerce were seen as incompatible with the demands of a virtuous life, and usury and gambling were strictly prohibited. In brief, individual life was subordinated to both the demands of salvation and the Church sponsored view of societal needs (Fusfeld, 1999, pp.7-27).

---

[1]    This concept of hierarchy and role was not necessarily a part of the teachings of Jesus Christ (pbuh) but a later religious legitimization of feudal social surroundings (MacIntyre, 1966, p.116).

## THE MODERN QUEST FOR JUSTICE

In general, the roots of the modern Western quest for discovering reason-based principles of justice go back to the end of the Middle Ages. That period saw the rise of the modern nation state through intense conflict: (a) between rival views on organizing society, (b) the competing jurisdictional claims of the Church, feudal barons, and medieval parliaments against monarchs, and (c) the external struggle for conquest under the influence of mercantilism. Under the circumstances, there was a clear arbitrariness in distributing social dividends and burdens that prompted social philosophers to ask: how can an orderly and harmonious social system emerge from the pursuit of competing self interests? How can social organization be redeemed from warring concepts of common good? And, how can individuals be protected against arbitrary state action and confiscation? The erstwhile Greek and Christian traditions, albeit helpful, did not provide satisfactory answers. In any case, splits in opinion among the clergy challenged whatever commitment remained to that vision. Under these circumstances, two influences are said to have played a key role in forging a new ethics of equality and liberalism. First, the Islamic and, second, the Roman tradition. As regards the former, Wells (1961) writes:

> And a century or so in advance of the West, there grew up in the Moslem world at a number of centres, at Basra, at Kufa, at Baghdad and Cairo, and at Cordoba, out of what were at first religious schools dependent upon mosques, a series of great universities. The light of these universities shone far beyond the Moslem world, and drew students to them from east and west. At Cordoba in particular there were great numbers of Christian students, and the influence of Arab philosophy coming by way of Spain upon the universities of Paris, Oxford, and North Italy, and upon Western European thought generally, was very considerable indeed. (p.626)

Robinson (1996) also confirms:

> recent scholarship has come to find the roots of medieval scholasticism and the development of universities in Muslim influence. It has even gone so far as to find the origins of Renaissance humanism in that of classical Islam. 'I have read, reverend fathers', Pico della Mirandola begins his oration The Dignity of Man in the late fifteenth century, 'that when Abdala the Saracen was asked what he regarded as most to be wondered at on the world stage ... he answered that there was nothing to be seen more wonderful than man.' (p.xxi)

Insofar as Roman influence is concerned, this came through their civil code. The Roman code, as presented in a sixth-century document, *Corpus iurus civilis* compiled by Justinian, was primarily concerned with providing legal protection to commercial activity and private property without entertaining any given view of righteousness or virtue. The state, in this concept, was a privileged legal or constitutional order with sovereign jurisdiction over a geographical territory. These insights inspired the tradition of natural jurisprudence at the hands of Hugo Grotius (1583-1645), Thomas Hobbes (1588-1679), Samuel von Pufendorf (1632-1694), Baruch Spinoza (1632-77), and John Locke (1632-1704).[2] It was argued that individuals were to be considered as equal and ends in themselves rather than as means to the happiness of others. This was possible only if the state allowed the pursuit of pluralistic

---

[2]    A clarification is in order here. For Hugo Grotius and Pufendorf, the state was the result of a social contract derived from the moral precept of natural law. Hobbes abandoned natural law and based his contract instead on observations of human nature. Locke attempted to steer a course between the Aristotelian concept of the social nature of man and the increasingly popular individualistic theory of man devised by Hobbes (Musgrave, 1959, p.63).

concepts of good in a society, and placed minimal demand on individuals by respecting their rights and restricting the domain of their political obligations to what could be deduced from non-controversial rational premises, for example, self-preservation.

During the seventeenth and eighteenth centuries, these arguments turned the tide gradually in favour of viewing social order in terms of achieving the goals of freedom and opulence. Free market exchange began to be seen as preserving freedom and/or aligning these goals. As Kolm (1996, p.59) says, this tradition, called in its fully evolved form Libertarianism/Liberalism/Full-process freedom is the historically original, founding, and central theory of modernity.

### Libertarianism

Libertarianism stands for the type of social arrangements that guarantee each person the greatest amount of liberty commensurate with the same liberty for all (Sterba, 1992). But what does liberty stand for? Why has it to be the core value of a social order? What are the demands of liberty? How do these demands translate in terms of the role of government in a society? These are some of the questions that we examine below.

Liberty is important, it is said, because it constitutes the essence of our being. It reflects the agency aspect of a person's being in that it refers to what a person is free to do and achieve in terms of forming aims, objectives, allegiances, commitments, and plans of action in accordance with some overall concept of good that he chooses to value. It demonstrated that a person endowed with will can take actions that are caused by that will and influence the world. The more an action is caused in accordance with the will of a person, the freer that action is (Sen, 1985; Kolm, 1996, p.38).

Sen (1993) elaborates upon at least two aspects of the liberty to act. First, there is the opportunity aspect that refers to the real opportunities (means) that one has in order to achieve what one has reason to value. Second, there is a process aspect that refers to the freedom of aims and acts. It is this process aspect that has been the major concern of libertarians and that, in turn, consists of two elements: the autonomy of individual choices and immunity from interference by others. The crucial issue in case of autonomy is whether choices are being made by the person concerned rather than by other individuals and institutions on his behalf. For immunity, the focus usually is on 'negative freedoms', i.e. the absence of obstacles external to a person – coercion and legal prohibitions – that prevent wilful action.

Traditionally, libertarians have stressed the importance of negative freedoms by emphasizing that a person has inalienable rights to life, liberty, health, property (and this includes protection against theft, fraud, and breach of contract), the right to defend against violations of these rights, and the right to punish transgressors against these rights (Haslett, 1994, p.55). The economic implications of these rights are worthy of note. First, the distributional consequences of economic arrangements depend on the existing allocation of property rights. Thus the starting point for resource distribution has to be justified in some normative sense. Second, procedural rules for further entitlement have to be clarified in order to lower transaction costs, encourage investment, and mitigate socially wasteful effort. Third, the pursuit of certain economic goals has to be ruled out (Hausman and McPherson, 1996, pp.126-127). These requirements are catered for by rules of entitlement.

Locke, for example, considers natural resources as the common property of mankind but grants rights of entitlement to those who mix their labour with these resources. Occupancy is, thus, implied. However, spoilage and destruction are prohibited and enough and as good must be left for the rest. Above all, each person has a right to subsistence when others are living in plenty (Sugden, 1992, p.280). Nozick (1974) modifies this framework by omitting the right to subsistence. The rules of acquisition are re-interpreted to mean that an act of appropriation must not worsen the situation of others in terms of using (not owning) what they could previously. This opens up the way for the concentration of resources in a few hands on the grounds of higher productivity. Rectification of past unjust acquisitions is limited to living generations. And, voluntary transfers through bequest, gift, and trade are freely permitted. Nevertheless, certain important issues remain unexplained. Not least, according to Musgrave (1985), why earnings from capital have an entitlement claim *pari passu* with earnings from labour. Certainly, in a longer historical context, that claim was not taken for granted by many noteworthy scholars. Furthermore, is a voluntary exchange of rights, i.e. not through a competitive market, a sufficient condition for legitimate entitlement? What about transfers at death which do not constitute the fruit of the recipient's labour? Finally, how should externalities be dealt with?

From a libertarian standpoint, given initial property rights and a procedure for further entitlements, protection cannot be left as everybody's business. A civic society/government must be established to protect property. People join in, of their own accord, as free and equal. Financing of protection costs is on a *quid pro quo* basis. Such a 'night-watchman state' indulges neither in the provision of public goods nor in redistribution and any taxation for purposes other than a 'minimal' state is condemned as 'forced labour' (Nozick, 1974).

There are some differences among notable libertarians in terms of the defence of liberty. While for Nozick (1974), it derives from the prior idea of self-ownership, others take it for granted, derive a catalogue of rights from it, and then justify the market as the institution compatible with this concept. Still others, like Adam Smith, in his *The Wealth of Nations* published in 1776, reach libertarian conclusions not through the premises of rights – because historically rights have been an exception rather than the rule – but by emphasizing the centrality of competitive exchange in promoting opulence and freedom, and organizing international relations on a pacified footing. These insights provide the basis for Smith's vision of the role of government in society:

> Every man as long as he does not violate the laws of justice, is left perfectly free to pursue his own interest his own way, and to bring both his industry and capital into competition with those of any other man, or order of men. The sovereign is completely discharged from a duty, in the attempting to perform which he must always be exposed to innumerable delusions, and for the proper performance of which no human wisdom or knowledge could ever be sufficient; the duty of superintending the industry of private people, and of directing it towards the employments most suitable to the interests of the society. According to the system of natural liberty, the sovereign has only three duties to attend to; three duties of great importance, indeed, but plain and intelligible to common understandings: first the duty of protecting the society from the violence and invasion of other independent societies; secondly, the duty of protecting, as far as possible, every member of the society from the injustice or oppression of every other member of it, or the duty of establishing an exact administration of justice; and, thirdly, the duty of erecting and maintaining certain public works and certain public institutions, which it can never be for the interest of any individual, or small number of individuals, to erect and maintain; because the profit could never repay the expense to any individual or small number of individuals, though it may frequently do much more than repay it to a great society. (Smith [1776] 1966, pp.180-1).

Thus, in contrast with Nozick, some works of a public good nature are admitted in the government portfolio. Hayek (1976) too emphasizes the impossibility of planned action to replicate market efficiency in creating wealth as the reason for minimal government. Justice, in this view, requires 'equality before the law' and that may not result in the satisfaction of independent criteria for social justice such as reward according to merit, needs or effort. In fact, as Hayek says, liberty requires reward according to perceived value not according to merit. Assessing end states of a society is therefore a mirage of social justice. Hayek also wants all money to be private. Milton Friedman disagrees but only somewhat: he proposes small-scale redistribution through negative income tax, the finance of schooling with vouchers, and all money to be in the public domain (Rowley, 1993; Kolm, 1996, pp.349, 381).

In summary, libertarianism as a political philosophy of 'equal liberty for all' has been closely associated with championing the cause of *laissez-faire* capitalism and limiting the role of government to the protection of property rights. Libertarians consider that only individuals have means, values, plans and ends. Society has no ends apart from the ends of its individuals. Therefore, individuals alone ought to be taken as a basic unit in the analysis of social phenomenon (methodological and normative individualism).

The most common critique of libertarianism is that while free markets are important, they may not necessarily produce results that are compatible with liberty. Sen (1999, pp.64-67), for example, criticizes libertarianism on the grounds that its 'consequent-independent' stance provides too restricted an information base to encompass basic variables that human beings have a reason to value. Thus stark poverty and extreme hunger can exist precisely because people have libertarian rights but no right to nourishment which is a pre-condition for appreciating freedom. This means libertarianism is ultimately indifferent to achieving substantive liberty as an end. He raises the question as to why the status of economic needs, which can be a matter of life and death, should be lower than that of personal liberties?

## Socialist justice

We saw above that social arrangements based on a guarantee of negative freedoms are indifferent to the distribution of social product or the opportunity aspect of freedom. The practice of *laissez-faire* capitalism in eighteenth and nineteenth century England provided a window into what might happen under these circumstances. Sixteen-hour working days, child labour under brutality, and the struggle for the ordinary person to make ends meet in spite of such effort were 'all too illustrative of a social climate in which the practices of [the] most callous inhumanity were accepted as the natural order of events and even more important, as nobody's business' (Heilbroner, 1967, pp.96-97). Utopian socialist and Marxist thought was chiefly a product of that age. Karl Marx (1818-83 CE), in particular, questioned whether the supply of wage labour by propertyless workers was really free or forced. To him, workers who were paid subsistence wages were forced to work at that price because the alternative was starvation. This, he thought, was akin to slavery and implied a contradiction of the libertarian principle that a person was entitled to the full product of his labour. In fact, he argued, that it was in this phenomenon of compensating labour with less than what it was due, together with past accumulation by war, looting, or slavery wherein lied the source of exploitative capital accumulation. The solution he recommended was the abolition of private property (nationalization of the means of production) and the pursuit of the ultimate vision, 'from each according to his ability, to each according to his need'. This reminds us of Rousseau's (1712-78 CE) egalitarian ideal whereby, 'No one should have either so little as to have to sell himself or so much as to be able to buy someone else', (Kolm, 1996, pp.237-41). Some contemporary socialists recommend a route that is less radical. They call for spreading the ownership of the means of production through wider share ownership.

### Welfare liberal justice

The welfare liberal tradition takes a middle path between liberalism and Marxism: it recommends a combination of free markets, business regulation, and state sponsored redistribution. It emphasizes the opportunity aspect of freedom or the equal moral worth of each person. Arguably, the roots of this philosophy lie in the rules of Scripture, for example, do unto others as you would have them do unto you; all men are equal in the eyes of God; and love your neighbour as yourself. In political philosophy, Immanuel Kant – in his *Groundwork of the Metaphysic of Morals*, published in 1785 – devised a rational equivalent of these rules in the form of the universality of a moral principle. The aim of this tradition is to combine both liberty and equality into a political concept that derives from a fair social contract. Rawls (1971) has been the most influential contemporary philosopher in this tradition. Of course, many prior to him, in particular, utilitarian economists, have justified redistributive philosophy based on 'maximum utility' (Musgrave, 1985; Sterba, 1992). Below we examine each alternative in turn.

### Justice as fairness

Rawls (1971) considers justice as the first virtue of social institutions just as truth is of systems of thought. He then aims to determine the principles of justice for the basic structure of a society that is conceived as a system of fair co-operation between free, equal, and rational people each of whom has the twin moral powers of good and justice. The people are to choose, in one joint act, the principles that would guide the political constitution and the principal economic and social arrangement, viz., institutional structure, legislature, laws, rules, the distribution of social benefits and burdens, and all subsequent criticism and reform of institutions. Many social contract theories use different features of the (unfavourable) state of nature to instil willingness among parties to contract out of such a situation. However, the terms of co-operation conceived by each person may diverge from others owing to the pluralistic concept of good and positional advantage. What is needed is to abstract people from knowledge of their current and future position in society, endowments and natural abilities, degree of risk aversion, and other circumstances such as race, sex, political and economic situation. This is achieved by putting them behind a veil of ignorance. This veil also simulates the likelihood that the post-contract person may end up having any combination of natural endowments and social status bringing home the consideration that the good of everyone else is one's own. Equality between people as moral agents is thus obtained.

Rawls argues that behind such a veil of ignorance, rational people will opt to minimize the risk of ending up in worse socio-economic circumstances. They, thus, choose the following principles of justice:

1. Each person is to have an equal right to the most extensive total system of equal basic liberties compatible with a similar system of liberty for all;
2. Social and economic inequalities are to satisfy two conditions: first, they must be attached to offices and positions open to all under conditions of fair equality of opportunity; and second, they must be to the greatest benefit of the least advantaged members of society.

The first of these principles calls for right to political liberties, i.e. the right to vote, to be eligible for public office, freedom of speech and assembly, freedom of thought, liberty of conscience, freedom from arbitrary arrest and confiscation, and the right to hold property. The second of these is called the difference principle. It allows inequalities only on the condition that they work to the benefit of those with fewer resources, for example, by providing incentives for the talented / resourceful to use their endowments in a socially beneficial manner (the mini-max principle). This does not allow any amount of gain to the better-off if it is achieved at a cost to the worst-off. Together, these principles ensure a set of primary goods for each person that are required at minimum to form and pursue private goals.

Rawls also provides an alternative justification for the above difference principle based on equal opportunity: he appeals to our intuition that morally arbitrary inequalities are unfair. Ordinarily, such inequalities are considered to consist of differences in race, sex, or social background. It is thought that if the political and social structure equalizes these disadvantages so that they do not have a bearing on the pursuit of education, political office, or occupation in society, then, receiving unequal rewards is acceptable given fair competition. Rawls challenges this notion on the grounds that no one 'deserves' to be born with exceptional talents any more than they 'deserve' to be born in socially advantaged / disadvantaged households. The common concept of equal opportunity is, therefore, unstable because it seeks to address the differences in the distribution of social goods owing to social disadvantages but ignores differences owing to talents, although from a moral perspective both are beyond one's control and arbitrary in nature. With reference to this premise, then, the difference principle is justified in admitting distributional inequality of any kind only if it is to the benefit of those who are disadvantaged in any manner (pp.219-222).

What are the implications of this view for the institutional structure of an economy? To quote Rawls:

> Since under socialism the means of production and natural resources are publicly owned, the distributive function is greatly restricted, whereas a private-property system uses prices in varying degrees for both purposes. Which of these systems and the many intermediate forms most fully answers to the requirements of justice cannot, I think, be determined in advance. ... it depends in large part upon the traditions, institutions, and social forces of each country, and its particular historical circumstances. ... The political judgement in any given case will then turn on which variation is most likely to work out best in practice. (pp. 273-74).

Nevertheless, the social system is to be designed so that the resulting distribution is just however things turn out. This implies some view of human good that is implicit in the principles of justice to be realized through the design of institutions. The call therefore is to consider a blend of moral, political, and economic criteria in designing institutions that actualize principles of justice as fairness (pp.259-60). Efficiency, in this scheme, provides too narrow a basis for such design. In the event, it is conceived that government should balance different claims by having (a) an allocation branch, (b) a stabilization branch, (c) a transfer branch and (d) a distribution branch. The allocation branch promotes competitive markets that are necessary for preserving incentives to create wealth and the stabilization branch aims at achieving full employment. But markets give little consideration to needs and an appropriate standard of life. Markets are, therefore, supplemented with distribution of a 'suitable minimum' through the transfer branch. Finally, the distribution branch aims at gradually correcting wealth distribution with the view that its concentration does not reach the level detrimental to the very institutions that are to ensure the 'fair value' of political liberties and so the equality of opportunity incorporated in principles of justice is maintained.

Rawls' concept of justice differs from others on a number of accounts. First, his position that all inequalities are morally arbitrary is in direct conflict with the libertarian argument of self-ownership, i.e. that individuals have an unfettered right to the usufruct of themselves. Second, Rawls' focus on primary goods, goods that any rational person will want regardless of his preferences is at odds with utilitarianism that aims at advancing the aggregate utility of a community's members. Finally, Rawls' justice as fairness is not a comprehensive ethical theory but rather a (common) political concept that leaves each individual to choose his own concept of good (Sugden, 1992).

Rawls' articulation has been criticized on many accounts. Among others that there is a need to differentiate among inequalities that result from people's choice from those that result from people's circumstances (Dworkin, 1981). In practice, however, it is not easy to identify such differences.

*Utilitarian justice*

Utilitarianism has dominated moral and political philosophy, economics, and public policy for more than a century. It stands for the type of social arrangements that maximize aggregate utility whereas utility, in its Benthamite interpretation, depicts the tendency of an action/law/institutional arrangement to augment happiness. And although pleasure and happiness are essentially mental characteristics that defy precise measurement, it is not considered absurd to relate them to maximizing some observable economic characteristic, for example, income, that is a means to achieving many aims. The idea is to shift the foundations of public action from religion and natural laws to some secular and scientific basis. And utility is central to that notion because it is committed neither to an *a priori* concept of human nature nor to a specific role of government. In the words of Bentham (1789):

- 'Nature has placed mankind under the governance of two sovereign masters, pain and pleasure. It is for them alone to point out what we ought to do, as well as to determine what we shall do. On the one hand the standard of right and wrong, on the other the chain of causes and effects, are fastened to their throne.

- ... The principle of utility is the foundation ... that principle which approves or disapproves of every action whatsoever, according to the tendency which it appears to have to augment or diminish the happiness of ... the party whose interest is in question ... not only of every action of a private individual, but of every measure of government.

- ... A measure of government (which is but a particular kind of action, performed by a particular person or persons) may be said to be conformable to or dictated by the principle of utility, when in like manner the tendency which it has to augment the happiness of the community is greater than any which it has to diminish it.

- ... Of an action that is conformable to the principle of utility one may always say either that it is one that ought to be done, or at least that it is not one that ought not to be done. One may say also, that it is right it should be done; at least that it is not wrong it should be done: that it is a right action; at least that it is not a wrong action. When thus interpreted, the words ought, and right and wrong, and others of that stamp, have a meaning: when otherwise, they have none.' (Chapter 1: Of the Principle of Utility, p.1 ff.)

As Sen (1999, pp.58-59) explains, the informational content of justice so conceived can be split into three components: consequentialism, welfarism, and sum-ranking. Consequentialism requires that all choices among alternative courses of action – including rules, institutions, policies – be made on the basis of the goodness of the states of affairs that they generate. This rules out actions based on norms of righteousness that disregard consequences. Welfarism stands for evaluating the goodness of a state of affairs on the basis of the corresponding utility information. This principle does not recognize the direct bearing of information such as the fulfilment or violation of rights and duties on the evaluation or decision making process. And, sum-ranking requires that the utilities of different people in a group or society be simply added together to arrive at the total utility – social utility – corresponding to a state of affairs. This requirement is indifferent to the distribution of individual utilities. The net result of the three components is that every choice is to be judged by the sum total of utilities generated through that choice.

Sen's statement that norms of righteousness do not directly influence utility information reflects to a degree the long standing struggle in the utilitarian doctrine to find a plausible meaning for 'utility'. The idea is that the content of utility should be broad enough to encompass the condition of human mind, not incorporate a particular view of the good, be measurable, and provide guidance on public policy. Pleasure or desire fulfilment versions of utility have difficulty in satisfying all these criteria (Sugden, 1992, p.265). Bentham himself resolved the tension in at least three ways. First, he distinguished between the agenda of the government, the non agenda, and *sponte acta*, that is, actions which individuals could be relied upon to undertake spontaneously. Second, he listed four objectives of public policy: subsistence, security, abundance, and equality, ranked in that order, and at times rivalrous (Spiegel, 1971, p.342). Third, he equated pleasure with wealth and floated the principle of the diminishing marginal utility of wealth implying that total happiness increased with equality of wealth. However, such equality when in conflict with security must yield to the latter. In other words, inequality can be reduced but not eliminated. Thus the principle of the greatest happiness for the greatest number did not commit Bentham to *laissez-faire* but rather to a substantial role for legitimate government activities (Musgrave, 1985).

The utilitarian research programme over the two hundred years since Bentham has focused primarily on refining the Benthamite framework of analysis and widening its application. For example, J. S. Mill in his *Principles of Political Economy*, published in 1848, argued for expanding the role of government to natural monopolies, public goods (education, the care of neglected children and provision for the poor and mentally retarded), and the promotion of speculative knowledge. He also made an important departure from the classical economics of Ricardo and Malthus by differentiating between production and distribution. For production, *laissez-faire* was probably the best but for distribution, the socialist approach was attractive. Accordingly, Mill argued:

> no rational person will maintain it to be abstractly just, that a small minority of mankind should be born to the enjoyment of all the external advantages which life can give ... while the immense majority are condemned from their birth to a life of never-ending, never intermitting toil, requitted by a bare, and in general a precarious subsistence. (quoted in Fusfeld, 1999, p.53)

The solution that he recommended was workers' co-operatives and profit sharing schemes. Henry Sidgwick (1838-1900), another economist in the utilitarian tradition, took issue with socialism, in his *The Principles of Political Economy*, on the grounds of its incompatibility with individual incentives and the potential loss in overall national product, (Usher, 1992, pp.55-59). However, he warned that under certain conditions, *laissez-faire* would not produce the acclaimed results. These conditions included: the use of wealth to gratify the lust for power, i.e. by influencing the minds of the less well-off, the presence of externalities, worker or enterprise monopolies, inadequate consumer information, advertising, and public goods. The scope for public sector intervention in each case depended on the potential for correction given corruption, special interest politics, wasteful public expenditure, the social cost of taxation and regulation, and the absence of incentives in government to match the enthusiasm and interest of a private stakeholder. Sidgwick also provided a list of economic exceptions to *laissez-faire*: moral considerations such as sanitary regulations, the control of narcotics and intoxicants, and restrictions on gambling; efforts to improve the productivity of individuals by education; measures that require total public participation for effectiveness, such as public health measures and flood control; and the provision of services whose benefits are general and for which the individual cannot be charged, such as lighthouses on rocky shores or certain types of scientific research (Fusfeld, 1999, p.96).

The utilitarian influence on public economics reached a high in the hands of A. C. Pigou (1877-1959). Pigou (1918) introduced a rationale for government intervention in correcting externalities and proposed the imposition of what became known as Pigouvian taxes (subsidies) to obtain efficient allocation. He also demonstrated that because of its failure to assess social costs, the market mechanism tended to misallocate resources between increasing-cost and decreasing-cost industries. Pigou's most controversial demonstration, however, was the justification for income redistribution on utilitarian grounds based on the following assumptions: the utility that a person derives from any thing is cardinally measurable; utilities of different individuals can be measured in the same units, say utils; all individuals have similar tastes. Accordingly, the marginal satisfaction that individuals say, having the same initial total income, derive from a given increase in income, is the same; income has diminishing marginal utility. Thus a rich person enjoys an additional dollar worth of income comparatively less than a poor person. Income transfers from the rich to the poor therefore increase the 'aggregate sum of satisfaction' and, hence, social welfare.

Although the assumptions that Pigou floated had been echoed throughout the history of utilitarianism, in the hay days of logical positivism, they created a stir. In particular, Lionel Robbins (1935) took the stand that it was not 'scientific' to compare one person's utility with another. Citing W. S. Jevons, who wrote, 'every mind is inscrutable to every other mind and no common denominator of feelings is possible', he argued that interpersonal comparisons of utilities was tantamount to ethical judgements that had no role in economic policy. Research on value free economics that followed as a result ultimately reduced the information base of utilitarianism to the Pareto criteria.

Utilitarianism has been criticized on a number of accounts. First, that it reduces both what is good and just to the maximization of utility. This view that utility is all that matters, and that any other intrinsic good that people value is irrelevant or relevant only to the extent that it is reflected in their utility, flies in the face of many widely agreed right-based and need-based theories of human welfare. Rights, as we saw above, are important because they define personhood and are also the defining point of economic exchange. In the absence of recognizing rights, it is conceivable that utilitarianism would not bar forced slavery if the loss to the utility of the would-be slave was outweighed by the gain to the utility of the master. Furthermore, it would not prohibit people from willingly selling themselves into bondage under appalling conditions (Holcombe, 1998, p.13).[3] Thus it can be argued that utility – both in its 'happiness' and 'desire fulfilment' versions – neither adequately represents well-being nor is well-being so defined as the only thing that is valuable in real life (Sen, 1987, p.46). Second, in oppressed and disadvantaged communities, happiness or desire satisfaction may itself adjust downwardly making utility an inadequate measure of well-being (Sen, 1999, pp.62-63). Third, although the utility theory does not make any claims of a substantive nature about what people should prefer, it is still a normative theory because it lays down conditions that choices and preferences ought to satisfy. In particular, in order to identify well-being with preference satisfaction, individuals are presumed as rational, self-interested and well-informed, and their preferences are considered as not being deformed in odd ways as through advertising. These assumptions are taken for granted and there is little work on preference formation or preference satisfaction automatically leading to well-being. Thus in practice, the preference satisfaction view of welfare acts as a veil behind which economists can impose their own paternalistic preferences on society, in particular on matters such as merit wants. This introduction of value judgements from the back door imparts on utilitarian ethics a strong flavour for social engineering that has historically been used to justify an activist and radicalist role for government (Rowley, 1993).

In summary, it can be argued that partly in search of attaining the greatest happiness for the greatest number and partly due to the influence of socialist thought, utilitarianism gradually drifted public economics away from the classical liberal notion of limited government. Although a commitment to private property remained,

---

[3]    This objection is taken care of by a variant called rule utilitarianism, i.e. only those rules are acceptable that apply uniformly to all members of society.

varying degrees of redistribution were favoured and an expanding role of government was envisaged under varying degrees of market failure.

## THE ISLAMIC THEORY OF JUSTICE

### *Background*

The Arabia into which the Prophet Muḥammad (pbuh) was born in 570 CE had no central authority akin to a state. The vacuum was filled to some extent by clans/tribes who prized their independence. A tribe was headed by a senior person known as *shaykh*. A *shaykh* would resolve intra-tribal matters through a mix of mutual consultation, custom, and moral persuasion. He usually had no enforcement mechanisms *per se* at his disposal; the mere subsistence level economy in the desert levelled all differences among people. In this sense, a desert Arab (*Bedouin*) was a born democrat (Hitti, 1970). However, the situation in commercial towns such as Makkah was different. Here, markets operated freely and great differences in wealth left the poor, orphans, and women at the receiving end of exploitation and injustice (Esposito, 1995, pp.28-9).

Given the absence of a central authority and proximity to the 'state of nature', inter-tribal conflicts were frequent. Against this backdrop, the most common notion of fairness known among the Arabs was tantamount to retributive justice, which consisted of taking revenge. A peaceful alternative to this, *diyah* or blood money was also admitted depending on the need for survival and strength in bargaining. The following quote from El-Awa (1983) is self-explanatory:

It was by no means rare for small disputes to turn into an actual war between two tribes; for example, the war between the tribes of Banū Bakr and Banū Taghlib lasted for forty years because one of the Banū Taghlib killed a female camel belonging to a women of the Banū Bakr. An attempt at a peace settlement was made after the son of a distinguished Arab, Shās b. Zuhayr b. Judhaymah, was killed, but the father asked the representative of the killer's tribe to do one of three things in order to stop him from taking revenge for his son: to return his son to life, to fill his garment (*ridā'*) with the stars, or to hand over to him all the members of the killer's tribe to be killed. "Still", the father added, "I will not be compensated for my son." (p.70)

It can be argued from this picture of pre-Islamic Arabia that individuals keenly defended negative freedoms of their own and their tribesmen but respected little of the same for others. The Holy Qur'ān attributes this state of affairs to corruption of reason, lack of faith, moral ignorance, and pride in ancestry, strength and riches, a condition frequently present in the history of mankind (91:7-10; 17:49-51; 34:31-6; 48:26; 9:69). Not surprisingly, the remedy suggested is no different: a renewal of the covenant made at the time of the fall of Adam (2:37-9) by admitting and implementing a revealed code of justice.[4]

---

4    Consider, for example, these verses: *We verily sent Our apostles with clear proofs, and sent down with them the Book and the Balance (of right and wrong) that men may stand forth in justice; and We sent down Iron in which is (material for) mighty war as well as many benefits for mankind that Allah may test who it is that will help unseen Him and His apostles; for Allah is Full of Strength exalted in Might (and able to enforce His will).* (57:25); *And this (He commands): Judge you between them by what Allah has revealed and follow not their vain desires but beware of them lest they beguile you from any of that (teaching) which Allah has sent down to you. And if they turn away be assured that for some of their crimes it is Allah's purpose to punish them. And truly most men are rebellious.* (5:49)

## Meaning

In general, the Holy Qur'ān uses three terms, *'adl* (justice), *qisṭ* (equity), and *mīzān* (balance/scale) to signify justice and equity. Among the meanings of these words are: to straighten, set in order, and fix in the right place; to balance, counterbalance, or establish equilibrium; to be equal or equivalent or to match; fairness, impartiality, absence of discrimination and, honesty, straightforwardness, uprightness, righteousness, and correctness. The antonym of *'adl* is *ẓulm*, which is used in the Holy Qur'ān (e.g., 2:124; 4:148) to mean indulgence in wrong, evil, iniquity, injustice, oppression, unfairness that eventuates in corruption (11:85) and sheer destruction (21:11). It also means darkness that beclouds and overshadows the truth (24:40; 57:9). Finally, the Holy Qur'ān (16:90; 3:134; 9:100, 120; 55:60; 5:93; 7:56; 2:195) stresses that *'adl* be complemented with *iḥsān* or benevolence.

The Qur'ān (e.g., 4:58, 105, 135; 5:8, 44-5, 48-50; 6:152; 7:29; 11:85; 16:90; 55:7-9; 57:25; 60:8) and *Sunnah* elucidate all these different dimensions of *'adl*, *qisṭ*, and *mīzān* with reference to both Divine attributes and the standards required of human beings while dealing with others. Insofar as justice as a manifestation of Divine Will is concerned, the Qur'ān (55:7) draws our attention to the heavens and reminds us figuratively that (1) justice is a heavenly virtue; (2) the heavens themselves are sustained by mathematical balance and (3) the constellation Libra (the Balance) is entered by the sun at the middle of the zodiacal year (see 55:7). The very next verses (55:8-9; 7:56) stress that there is a human equivalent to the just natural order established in the cosmos and that people ought to maintain it so as to have balance and equilibrium in their own lives and habitat. How is this human equivalent of natural balance (*'adl*) to be understood in Islam? On this issue, we examine four complementary perspectives.

We begin by pondering on the Qur'ānic position that it is the domain of God to elucidate the requirements of justice through prophets. Why is this so? The answer to this question derives from the purpose and nature of mankind discussed at length, again in revelation. To summarize, without revealed guidance, there is the potential for the corruption of reason owing to self-interest, short-termism, bounded rationality, and limited understanding of the relationship between *physis* and *nomos*.[5] Conversely, given immense potential attributed to reason to understand matter, albeit in an evolutionary manner, there is always a risk that some who control more 'matter' take complete charge of the rest of their own kind through devious means (again see 57:25) requiring such behaviour to be dealt with by an iron hand. If that happens, a person, created and dignified by God to act as His trustee on earth, cannot be made morally responsible for his/her actions given he/she is totally at the mercy of their captors. This is the reason why enslaving a free person is prohibited in Islam. Consider, for example, the following *ḥadīth*:

> The Prophet said, "Allah says, 'I will be against three persons on the Day of Resurrection: one who makes a covenant in My name, but he proves treacherous. One who sells a free person as a slave and eats the price. And one who employs a labourer and gets full work done by him but does not pay him his wages. [*Ṣaḥīḥ* of al-Bukhārī (*Ḥadīth*, 3.430)]

As Maudūdī (1962 [1994]) emphasizes, it is to save individuals from this eventuality that tribes, nations, and

---

5    That does not rule out the possibility of developing a rational framework that appears to work for a time for some or for many people. But, what we are concerned with in an Islamic context is 'justice for all' and of the kind that provides medium to long term peace, stability and equilibrium across the network of relations that man is a part.

international forums come into being. Thus, individuals do not live for society; rather, it is the society that comes into being for the sake of individuals. The idea is to provide people with the necessary security and patronage so that they can develop their full potential as free individuals and procure the needs and demands of their body and soul without violating the liberty of others. It is this violation of liberty that the *Sharī'ah* intends to protect individuals from. This position, we may argue, is supported by the following *hadīth*:

> Usāmah ibn Sharīk narrates that he was in the company of the Prophet Muhammad (pbuh) when Bedouins were asking him questions about sin. They asked him: 'Are we sinful if we do not seek treatment in case of illness?' He replied: 'O servants of God, God has not made anything sinful except that a person violates the honour/rights of his fellow men. This is (a greater) sin.' They again asked: 'Do we commit a sin, if we do not take medicine?' He replied: 'O men of God, I ordain you to seek treatment since there is no illness for which there is no cure except old age.' They asked: 'What is the best that a man can have?' He replied: 'Best manners (being good in dealing with others).' (*Sunan* of Ibn Mājah)[6]

In the distant past, al-Ghazālī and al-Shātibī did some original research on how the *Sharī'ah* is geared to achieving this task of protection. Zarqa (1980) and Siddiqi (1996) provide a glimpse of their works. In summary, the thesis is that underneath the metaphysical, eschatological and doctrinal content of the Qur'ān, lay the nitty-gritty of a justifiable blueprint of political, economic and social order. The starting point for reflection on such an order

---

[6]   Cited in Arshad, Malik Muhammad. 1994. *Mashhūr Hadīsen*. Rawalpindi, Pakistan: Naumi Publications: p.14. Referred further to *Sunan* of Ibn Mājah, Volume 3, Number 321.

is that wonderful creature, the human being, who has been created to become the trustee of God on earth. In this capacity, his pursuit of diverse intermediate ends is regulated through the *Sharī'ah* to ensure broad-based human welfare (*falāḥ*). The *Sharī'ah* achieves this goal by defining the sphere of liberties-and-violations/rights-and-responsibilities associated with the following pursuits that together constitute and define the whole struggle of life:

- *dīn* (religion);
- *nafs* (life);
- *'aql* (intellect or reason);
- *nasl* (family), and
- *māl* (property).

The concept of limits (*ḥudūd*: 9:12) set by God on individual freedoms in these areas is critical. These limits are set so as to promote *maṣāliḥ* (social utilities), i.e. all activities or things that help achieve these goals equitably and prohibit *mafāsid* (disutilities), which detract from (justly) obtaining these goals. Should there be a conflict of interest, there are other rules such as that of reciprocity (55:60) and precedence to help resolution.

This brings us to the second perspective on the issue of understanding *'adl* in Islam which is elaborated by Tahir-ul-Qadri (1995, p.86). He views the Qur'ānic stress on *'adl* in human conduct in light of the condition of faith mentioned in the Prophet's saying: 'I swear by the Lord Who controls my life that a person is not a true believer unless he likes for his brother what he likes for himself' [*Ṣaḥīḥ* of al-Bukhārī (*Ḥadīth*, 1.12)]. Thus justice consists of those principles which one would like to apply to one's own self if in a similar situation. Qadri then contrasts *'adl* with *iḥsān* in detail. We summarize the discussion below in Table 1.2 where *'adl* is distinguished from *iḥsān*.

### Table 1.2: *'Adl* (justice) and *iḥsān* (benevolence)

| *'Adl* (justice, equity) | *Iḥsān* (benevolence, kindness) |
|---|---|
| 1.    Equity is to give as much as is due and to take as much as is due.[7] | Benevolence is to give more than is due and to take less than is due. |
| 2.    Equity is that one should enjoy oneself and let others enjoy themselves as well. | Benevolence is that one should sacrifice one's sense of personal enjoyment for the enjoyment of others. |
| 3. It is equity that one should live for oneself as well as for others. | It is benevolence that one should live only for others (e.g. the Prophets of God mentioned in the Qur'ān, Ch. 28). |
| 4. Equity is equality and the condition of faith. | Benevolence is unconditional sacrifice and the perfection of faith. |

On this issue, Yusuf Ali's (*The Holy Qur'ān*, p.760) interpretation too is noteworthy. He argues that while justice is a comprehensive term, and may include all the virtues of cold philosophy, religion asks for benevolence which is something warmer and more humane. It calls for the doing of good deeds even where perhaps they are not strictly demanded by justice. This means, returning good for ill, obliging those who in worldly language 'have no claim' on you, and of course *a fortiori* the fulfilling of the claims of those whose claims are recognized in social life. Similarly the opposites are to be avoided, in particular the deeds described in the Qur'ān (16:90) as shameful and unjust, and any inward rebellion

---

7    This point is referred further to Imām Rāghib's *Al-Mufradāt*.

against Allah's Law or our own conscience in its most sensitive form.

It can be argued from the above table and discussion that at least in its external form, this understanding of justice comes very close to the Golden Rule to which the Western Kantian or welfare liberal concept of justice refer. Note, however, that as Musgrave (1985) states, the Golden Rule as an exclusive basis for deriving a theory of justice results in an asking for an equal division of the cake. That, under normal circumstances, would come under benevolence from an Islamic perspective rather than justice. The balancing act is another saying by the Prophet Muḥammad (pbuh): 'Gabriel kept on commending the neighbour to me so that I thought he would make him an heir', [Abū Dāwūd (Ḥadīth, 5133)]. Nevertheless, this was not done. Furthermore, the blueprint of justice is, as such, specified in the Sharī'ah rather than left for human reason to speculate from a single principle or two.

The third perspective on 'adl is presented by Smirnov (1996). He argues that 'adl equated with the straight path (al-ṣirāṭ al-mustaqīm) of the Qur'ān[8] can be understood as the middle path between two extremes where both get the best chance to display their spirit, the opposition between the two is neutralized, and harmony and unity emerge. Thus justice suffers when the exactness of 'preserving the middle' is lost through a twist one way or the other. This interpretation is supported by a saying of the Prophet Muḥammad (pbuh), 'Khayrul-umūri awsaṭuhā: the middle path (in things/commands/matters) is the best.' We may add that this principle can be deduced directly from the Qur'ān (2:143) that refers to the community of [practising] Muslims as 'the middle (justly balanced) nation' and, therefore, the 'best nation' (3:110). Seen from this angle, there is a common cord with the Aristotelian

---

8    See, for example, 6:151-53; 16:76.

interpretation of justice mentioned above, i.e. justice is a mean between the two extremes.

Finally, there is a fourth perspective that is also presented by Smirnov (1996). He argues that keeping all the different dimensions that the concepts of *'adl*, *qisṭ* and *mīzān* imbue, Muslim scholars throughout history have emphasized that justice in the secular definition of 'giving what is due', assumes in Islam, the character of "establishing the right (*ḥaqq*) in its due place (*makān*), to give [back] the really necessary to the one to whom it should belong, having taken it away from the usurper". This interpretation applied, for example, to the system of holding power and exercizing rule focuses not merely on the 'right' of a single person, group, community, or ruling person – regarded as separate units – but instead on *al-ḥaqq*, i.e. both the rights and obligations that make sense only within the overall network of linkages that unite the whole system. Such unity comes about by submitting to the certainty that flows from the absolute knowledge of the Divine Law-Giver, Who is the primary, correct, true, and everlasting basis for all subsequent links to the system. Thus, *ḥaqq*, in Islam, unites a 'right' through truth and righteousness with an 'obligation' so that they come together and imply each other by ontological and epistemological transitions and transformations necessary to establish balance, harmony, and equilibrium. And, *Sharīʿah* methodology (based on the Qurʾān, *Sunnah*, *ijmāʿ* and *ijtihād*) plays a key role in guiding reason to deduce these transitions and transformations.

## Content

It was mentioned above that the structure of Islamic *Sharīʿah* focuses on protecting the foundations of a good life through specifying a rights-obligations framework in relation to religion, life, intellect, family, and property. It is not possible to elaborate within a limited space all the different dimensions of this blueprint. Below, we limit our investigation to four aspects of the Islamic theory of justice that have an important bearing on the economic role of the state and its institutional architecture. These are, first, the concept of equality, second, the state-citizen relationship, third, economic and property rights, and fourth, welfare rights and obligations. Our views on these issues derive from the Islamic position on the dignity of human beings by virtue of their trusteeship[9] and the responsibilities that come with that role owing to unique capacities given to fulfill the demands of that office.

### Equality, brotherhood, and the mission of Muslims

A study of the Qur'ān and *Sunnah* makes it clear that human equality is the fundamental tenet of Islam. Consider, for example, the following verses from the Qur'ān:

> *O mankind! Lo! We have created you male and female, and have made you nations and tribes that you may know one another. Lo! the noblest of you, in the sight of Allah, is the best in conduct. Lo! Allah is Knower, Aware. (49:13). O mankind! Be careful of your duty to your Lord Who created you from a single soul and from it created its mate and from them both has spread abroad a multitude of men and women. Be careful of your duty toward Allah in Whom you claim (your rights) of one another, and toward the wombs (that bore you). Lo! Allah has been a Watcher over you. (4:1)*

---

9    In support, we cite the Qur'ān (17:70): *Verily We have honoured the children of Adam. We carry them on the land and the sea, and have made provision of good things for them, and have preferred them above many of those whom We created with a marked preferment.*

Thus Islam stresses that the apparent diversity in race, colour, language, and even religion veils a much deeper basis for co-operation among mankind, viz., that all are part of a single brotherhood by virtue of common origin. This brotherhood is re-asserted from many different angles. Three aspects are worthy of note. First, it is stressed that the external forms of rituals apart, the ideational aspect – core beliefs and values – of all religions is one (22:67). Thus religion *per se* ought not be the basis for disunity but rather for unity in competing for actualizing the good in life (2:140). Second, in conformity with this philosophy of equality and brotherhood, arrogance and defamation of fellow human beings – consisting in suspicion, spoken or written offences against individual or group titles, nicknames, and false propaganda – is prohibited (49:11-13). Third, there is this categorical emphasis on holding the hands of all those (people/communities/nations) who seek peace through abiding by a contract against mutual hatred, aggression, and deceit (25:63; 4:90; 8:61). This principle of reciprocity provides a firm foundation for inter-national relations. The objective is to establish a just and equitable world order based on principles of mutual respect, tolerance, and justice. The community of Muslims is required to play a special role in bringing out such order. In this context, there is this emphasis on another level of brotherhood (among Muslims) based on common beliefs, values, symbols, and mission. Thus the Prophet Muḥammad (pbuh) emphasized in his farewell pilgrimage:

> Behold! all practices of paganism and ignorance are now under my feet. The blood-revenge of the Days of Ignorance (pre-Islamic time) is abolished ... Usury is forbidden ... Fear Allah concerning women! Verily you have taken them on the security of Allah ... O people! beware! Your God is One, no Arab has any superiority over a non-Arab, and no non-Arab any superiority over an Arab, and no white one has any

superiority over a black one, and no black one has any superiority over a white one, except on the basis of *taqwā* (fear/love of Allah or piety).[10]

The purpose of Islamic brotherhood is to exemplify Islam by presenting a living picture to the world of the concepts of *tawḥīd*, justice, and benevolence (3:110; 2:143; 49:10). Bhutto (1976) is most perceptive in reminding us of the political significance of such teachings:

> ... our vocation as Muslims is not to harbour hostility against other human communities, East or West, North or South, but to conduct ourselves [so] that we can help build bridges of communication and sympathy between one set of nations and another. We draw our inspiration from the Holy Qur'ān and I quote: *"Say: To Allah belong both East and West: He guideth whom He will to a straight path. Thus We have appointed you a midmost nation that you might be witnesses over the nations and the Apostle a witness over yourselves."* [2:142-43]
>
> In being called the midmost nation or the People of the Middle, we are charged with the mission of mediating conflicts, spurning the doctrines of bigotry and hate, trampling underfoot the myths of racial or cultural superiority and translating into social terms the concepts of mercy and beneficence which constitute the core of our faith.
>
> The concept of the People of the Middle is suggestive also of a new synthesis. Through a conventional opposition, the East has been contemplative and the West, materialistic and

---

[10]   The last sermon of the Prophet Muḥammad (pbuh) is available in books of *Ḥadīth, Sīrah* (i.e. the life of Muḥammad) and also on some internet sites. This excerpt is compiled from *Ṣaḥīḥ* of Muslim (*Ḥadīth*, 2803.1) and from the internet site: *URL:* <http://www.usc.edu/dept/MSA/fundamentals/prophet/lastsermon.html> (Access date: 26 June 2000).

pragmatic. Islam rejects such dichotomies. The Muslim accepts both worlds, the spiritual and the material. What he tries to do is to find the reserves of spirituality, the respect for human personality and the sense of what is sacred in all cultural traditions, which could serve to fashion a new type of man. His aim is more than the mere mastery of Nature. If he is a true Muslim, he is at once Eastern and Western, materialistic and spiritual, a man of enterprise as well as of grace. (pp. 50-1)

How is the Islamic basis for equality and universal brotherhood to be actualized in a political set-up? This is the issue to which we now turn.

### The state-citizen relationship

As we saw above, the core of law in Islam is sacred, i.e. beyond the tempering of religious or temporal authorities. There is a detailed *Sharīʿah* structure in place to protect the five foundations of good life: faith, intellect, life, family, and property. This means even the state cannot encroach upon the freedoms and protections given in these areas (Chapra, 1992, p.208). Thus Lewis (1993) admits that the relationship between an Islamic state and its citizens is contractual in nature and subject to maintaining the *Sharīʿah* as the law of the land. This principle of the supremacy of the *Sharīʿah*, we should remember, flows directly from the Qur'ān and *Sunnah* and on it, throughout history, there has been an *ijmāʿ* (consensus) of Muslim scholars. The following advice by the Prophet Muḥammad (pbuh) on the occasion of the farewell pilgrimage is typical:

> If a slave with dark complexion and deformed limbs is appointed to govern over you and he conducts your affairs according to the Book of Allah, listen to him and obey his orders. [*Ṣaḥīḥ* of Muslim (*Ḥadīth*, 2977)].

What are the citizens' rights implicit in the Book of Allah in return for the obligation to support the *Sharī'ah*-abiding state/ruler through thick and thin? Iqbal (1986) illustrates this with an example from history:

> It is reported that one night while crossing a street of Madinah, the Caliph 'Umar heard sounds of debauchery coming from inside a house. He lost his temper and tried to enter the house, but no one answered his knock at the door. He climbed upon the roof and from it shouted down to the owner who was present in his lawn: "Why are you breaking the law and allowing such behavior in your house?" The man replied: "No Muslim has the right to speak to another in that manner. Maybe I have committed a wrong, but think how many wrongs you have committed. For instance: (1) spying – despite Allah's command 'thou shalt not spy'; (2) breaking and entering – you came in over the roof despite the command of Allah, 'enter a house by the door'; (3) entering without the owner's permission – in defiance of Allah's command: 'enter no house without the owner's permission'; (4) omitting the *salām* - though Allah has commanded 'enter no house without indicating that you are a friend and calling peace (*salām*) on those within'." 'Umar felt very embarrassed and withdrew saying: "Well, I forgive your wrong." The owner retorted: "That is your fifth infringement; for if you claim to be an executor of Islamic law, then how can you say that you forgive what Allah has condemned as a wrong?" [11] (p. 49)

Thus, Islam allows no interference or intrusion into the personal or family affairs of anyone. Furthermore, spying is forbidden in normal times even if there is a strong probability that something wrong is going on in someone's house. Having guaranteed freedom of action in the private space, the public space is then protected from

---

[11]    See, for example, Qur'ān (49:12, 2:189, 24:27, 61).

the exhibition of preferences that contradict the *Shari'ah* and could influence or undermine decent family values.

Note also that one aspect of human freedom is that on certain specific matters pertaining to law, non-Muslim citizens (*dhimmīs*: the protected ones) of an Islamic state are differently placed *vis-à-vis* Muslims. Consider the following advice of 'Umar ibn al-Khaṭṭāb, the second caliph, in his last moments (on his death bed):

> I warn you concerning those given protection by Allah and His Apostle (i.e. *dhimmīs*): fulfill their contracts; fight for them; and do not burden them with what is beyond their ability. [*Ṣaḥīḥ* of al-Bukhārī (*Ḥadīth*, 4.287)]

Traditionally, this has meant freedom of belief, religious rites, constructing worshipping places, following family laws, and maintaining culture (for example, while pork and alcohol are prohibited for Muslims, these are not for non-Muslims in an Islamic state). On these matters, equality means that *dhimmīs* are not obliged to follow the Islamic law but are instead guaranteed freedom to follow their own ways (5:47). In addition, unless under agreement, they cannot be forced against their will to render military service for an Islamic state that is otherwise compulsory for Muslims. Except these issues, all citizens receive the same treatment before the public law (including that of the *Sharī'ah* law such as for stealing, slander, and murder [*qiṣāṣ*]). In this respect, Islam grants no privileges to anyone including heads of states, members of the legislature, eminent citizens or ordinary people. This is clear from the Prophet Muḥammad's warning: "O people! The nations before you went astray because if a noble person committed theft, they used to leave him, but if a weak person among them committed theft, they used to inflict the legal punishment on him. By Allah, if Fāṭimah, the daughter of Muḥammad committed theft, Muḥammad would cut off her hand" [*Ṣaḥīḥ* of al-Bukhārī (*Ḥadīth*, 8.779)]. This brings us to the Islamic view on justice in property rights.

### Economic and property rights and obligations

Islam preserves an individual's right to acquire and have property (4:29). However, the test lies in seeking property through means that are not unjust to others. To elaborate, Islam preserves the Judaeo-Christian ban on fixed interest without distinction (2:275-9). Fixed interest is equated with *ẓulm*, which, as we mentioned above, is the converse of justice, i.e. oppression. In contrast, trade with mutual consent is made legitimate (2:275), the writing and witnessing of trade contracts is encouraged (2:282) and the fulfilment of promises is mandatory (2:177). Nevertheless, transactions containing *gharar*, i.e. elements of uncertainty as regards the possession, quality, quantity, price or delivery date of the goods being transacted are prohibited and so is outright gambling (5:90). Also, hoarding is disallowed; trading in pork and intoxicants is prohibited for Muslims (2:173, 219; 5:90), and deceit, bribery, pornography and prostitution (83:1-3; 17:32-9; 24:2) are considered as various manifestations of corruption that distort the socio-economic equilibrium. Subject to these far-reaching reforms, Islamic economic philosophy accepts the profit motive, protects lawfully gained private property, prohibits intervention in real-supply-and-demand driven market prices, and admits a market economy in general.

Against this larger context, earning one's livelihood and engaging in economic activity is considered obligatory and next only to devotional worship.[12] It is, thus, equated with seeking the bounties of Allah (16:14). Through it, human beings can test their potentialities, suffice their earthly requirements, and fulfill their

---

12    *Ḥadīth* from Suyūṭī, *Al-Jāmiʿ al-Ṣaghīr*, quoted in Chapra (1992).

obligations. Asceticism is discouraged[13] and begging is frowned upon unless one is desperate (57:27). Income through one's own labour is considered a means to befriending God[14] and trading within the Islamic ethical framework earns the Almighty's choicest blessings.[15] Naturally, such an all-embracing concept of worship does not prohibit engaging in business on the Islamic holy day, Friday, before and after congregational prayer (62:10).

## *Welfare rights and obligations*

Two concepts – that of the trusteeship of humankind and the brotherhood of all – are most relevant in elaborating the Islamic position on welfare rights and obligations. Trusteeship means that the ownership of all the physical and mental resources belongs in an absolute sense to God (19:40, 80). Anything produced by the use of these resources too therefore belongs to God. Another way of looking at this issue is that human beings are momentarily granted ownership to their usufruct, but that share in the usufruct of the forces of nature is far too great compared to what comes from people themselves. As a result, the Qur'ān reminds us that people's claims that 'We have been given it only on account of knowledge or effort or desert' are not tenable in an absolute sense (28:78-82; 18:32-44; 67:30; 17:66-9; 68:19-33; 27:60-66). Reality is that God enlarges the

---

13    'Umar ... passed by a group of Qur'ān-readers who were sitting with their heads bent down. He was told that they were *mutawakkilūn* (resigned to fate). Thereupon he exclaimed: No. Rather they are *muta'akkilūn*, i.e. parasites who consumed other people's money. The true *mutawakkil* is one who sows the seed and depends on Allah for its germination.' (Yusuf, 1988, p.17.)

14    'The Prophet Muḥammad (pbuh) said: 'Nobody has ever eaten a better meal than that which one has earned by working with one's own hands. The Prophet of Allah, David, used to eat from the earnings of his manual labour.' [*Ṣaḥīḥ* of al-Bukhārī, (*Ḥadīth*, 3286)]

15    'The truthful and honest merchant shall be with the Prophets, with the standard-bearers of truth and with the martyrs.' [Tirmidhī (*Ḥadīth*, 2796)]

livelihood for those whom He wills and restricts it for whom He wills (17:30; 30:37-9; 34:35-7; 34:39; 42:12). In that distribution furthermore, there is a test for mankind.[16] Consider, for example, the following *ḥadīth*:

> Allah's Apostle (peace be upon him) said: Verily, Allah, the Exalted and Glorious, will say on the Day of Resurrection: O son of Adam, I was sick but you did not visit Me. He will say: O my Lord, how could I visit You when You are the Lord of the worlds? Thereupon He will say: Didn't you know that a certain servant of Mine was sick but you did not visit him, and were you not aware that if you had visited him, you would have found Me by him? O son of Adam, I asked you for food but you did not feed Me. He will say: My Lord, how could I feed You when You are the Lord of the worlds? He will say: Didn't you know that a certain servant of Mine asked you for food but you did not feed him, and were you not aware that if you had fed him you would have found him by My side? (The Lord will again say:) O son of Adam, I asked you for something to drink but you did not provide Me with any. He will say: My Lord, how could I provide You with something to drink when You are the Lord of the worlds? Thereupon He will say: A certain servant of Mine asked you for a drink but you did not provide him with one, and had you provided him with a drink you would have found him near Me. [*Ṣaḥīḥ* of Muslim (*Ḥadīth*, 6232)]

Thus the test of the trusteeship of humankind lies in seeking the bounty of God (4:32; 43:32) and spending from it as ordained by God (17:26-7; 4:36-8; 2:177; 51:19).

---

16  *He it is Who has placed you as viceroys of the earth and has exalted some of you in rank above others, that He may try you by (the test of) that which He has given you. Lo! Your Lord is swift in prosecution, and lo! He is Forgiving, Merciful.* (6:165)

The actualizing of the second concept, that of the universal brotherhood of humankind, is most manifest in a *ḥadīth* narrated in the *Ṣaḥīḥ* of Muslim (2219) by Jarīr which depicts the Prophet Muḥammad's (pbuh) great unease (the colour of his face changed) on coming across a people stricken with poverty. He then called the people of Madinah reciting the Qur'ān (4:1), exhorting them to give freely until two heaps of eatables and clothes were piled up and the face of the Messenger (peace be upon him) began to glisten like gold (on account of joy).

Some may argue that the precedent set by the Prophet was a requirement of *iḥsān* (benevolence) and *birr* (virtue) rather than justice. Insofar as justice is concerned, the relevant question is that if after all that is said above about the obligation to earn, the protection of property rights and the moral exhortation to spend voluntarily on the poor, a person fails to attain basic needs, does Islam offer a positive right to minimal subsistence through redistribution? The short answer to this question is, yes, society is obliged to fulfill the basic needs of its members; basic needs being interpreted in the socio-economic context of society. As Chapra (1992) and Siddiqi (1996) state, on this issue, prominent jurists over the centuries and of the present age have full agreement. However, it can be argued that there are multiple sources to turn to in case of need. Thus the family, neighbourhood,[17] and state provide successively higher levels of resource to draw upon. In the case of the family, for example, children, parents, and near relatives have rights and obligations upon each other (31:14; 2:83, 180, 215; 4:7, 11, 33, 36, 135; 6:151; 17:23). Writing on one aspect of these

---

[17]   Mujāhid said that 'Abdullāh ibn 'Amr slaughtered a sheep and said: "Have you presented a gift from it to my neighbour (who was a Jew), for I heard the Apostle of Allah (peace be upon him) saying: 'Gabriel kept on commending the neighbour to me so much that I thought he would make him an heir?'" [Abū Dāwūd (*Ḥadīth*, 5133)]

obligations, Ashtor (1976, p.112) acknowledges that the Muslim law of (obligatory) inheritance resulted in frittering away the large properties and probably impeded the accumulation of capital in rich merchant families during the Middle Ages. As far as the responsibility of the state is concerned, needs are to be fulfilled through an obligatory religious due called *zakāh* levied on income and wealth. If *zakāh* does not suffice, additional taxes may be levied on the rich subject to the state itself not indulging in prodigal expenditure. Referring to such an obligation, 'Alī, the fourth caliph, is reported to have said:

> Allah has levied upon the rich among the Muslims, in their wealth, an amount that would suffice for the poor amongst them. If the poor starve or go unclad it is because of what their rich are doing. Beware, Allah the Mighty and the Exalted will take a tough account from them and punish them with a painful torment. [Siddiqi (1996, p.9) refers it further to al-Ṭabarānī's *al-Mu'jam al-Ṣaghīr* and Abū 'Ubayd's *Kitāb al-Amwāl*.]

This position is compatible with many verses in the Qur'ān that count charity as a part of faith and righteousness. Consider, for example, the Qur'ān (Sūrah 90):

> *I swear by this city (Makkah);*
> *And you are a freeman of this city;*
> *And by the begetter (i.e. Adam) and that which he begot (i.e. his progeny);*
> *Verily We have created Man (insān) into toil and struggle;*
> *Thinketh he that none hath power over him?*
> *He says (boastfully): "Wealth have I squandered in abundance!"*
> *Thinketh he that none beholdeth him?*
> *Have We not made for him two eyes?*
> *And a tongue and two lips?*
> *And shown him the two highways (good and evil/justice and*

*injustice)?*
*But he has made no attempt to walk on the highway that is steep*
*(i.e. that leads to goodness and success);*
*And what will make you know the path that is steep?*
*(It is:) freeing a neck (slave/bondsman);*
*Or the giving of food in a day of privation;*
*To an orphan near of kin;*
*Or to a poor in misery;*
*(Only) then will you be of those who believe and enjoin patience*
*(constancy and self-restraint) and do deeds of kindness and*
*compassion.*
*Such are the Companions of the Right Hand.*
*But those who reject Our Signs they are the (unhappy) companions*
*of the Left Hand.*
*On them will be fire vaulted over [i.e. wrath of God].*[18]

In brief, wealth acquired through legitimate means
('entitlement') is not an end in itself in Islam but a means to moral
and spiritual enrichment. This happens when it is spent voluntarily
in fulfilling the needs of fellow human beings. Only then are human
beings purified from miserliness, greed, and pride.

## Summary

To summarize, Islam views justice as the precondition for
preserving peace, equilibrium, and harmony on earth which are
essential in their own right as well as to enable humankind to
understand the demands of their position as the trustees of God on
earth. In terms of form, justice is understood as a set of pairs of
individual freedoms-and-limits, rights-and-obligations and *maṣāliḥ*-
and-*mafāsid* (social utilities and disutilities) elucidated by God
(16:116) through His prophets (7:157) so that human beings honour

---

[18]   See also Qur'ān (6:65).

the rights of their fellow beings and do not exploit them. Justice also needs complementing with benevolence so that in the words of Maudūdī (1994), the former removes conflict and bitterness from a society while the latter imparts grace and excellence to it by filling it with pleasant harmony and sweet accord. To implement justice, the state assumes a central role. First, it subjugates itself to the demands of justice by establishing an institutional framework that is based on the principles of the equality of all, respect for privacy, freedom of faith, freedom of expression, protection of minority rights, constraints on arbitrary state action, and consultation (shūrā) in state affairs. Second, it establishes a Sharī'ah framework for entitlement to income and wealth, and guarantees resulting economic and property rights. Third, it implements the redistributive system of Islam (zakāh) to guarantee minimal subsistence. Explaining the relationship between justice so perceived and the role of the state in implementing it, a renowned scholar of Islam, Ibn Taymiyyah once said, 'God upholds the just state even if it is unbelieving, but does not uphold the unjust state even if it is believing', and that, 'the world can survive with justice and unbelief, but not with injustice and Islam'. As Chapra (1992, p.209) elaborates, injustice and Islam are at variance with each other and by their very nature, one of these has to uproot or weaken the other in order to survive and remain strong.

So how then does this concept compare with the different traditions within Western thought?

### Islam and the West: a comparison

While comparing the Islamic approach to justice with the different Western approaches, the first thing to be said is that we have deliberately avoided delving into different mental constructs – for example, the state of nature, the veil of ignorance, the social contract and the like, designed by diverse philosophers in arriving at principles of a just socio-political order. At one level, our reluctance to discuss these devices stems from our extensive awareness of their published critique in failing to facilitate concrete and uncontroversial outcomes. To the extent that such critique is admitted, the claim that these models can exude a superior alternative to religion is not tenable. At another level, it can be argued that these devices appear to be plagiarizing the very source that they tend to discredit (i.e. religion). To wit, it is not a secret that many treatises claiming Divine origin frequently invoke covenants and contracts: between God and human beings 'behind the veil' (7:172; 20:115), between God and prophets (3:81), among God, prophets and their communities (2:40, 63; 5:7-14, 70), and among human beings (4:21; 8:58; 9:7-12). So much so that the 'Divine prophecy' (2:30-38) portrays human beings denying such covenants as engaged in bloodshed and pillage on earth, a scene no different than that depicted later in Hobbes' state of nature. Notwithstanding these passing remarks on mental constructs, shunning their use in this monograph is expected to provide a pragmatic focus on the content of competing views on justice rather than on their real or heuristic origination, the use of which remains the precinct of an extremely sophisticated Platonic elite!

Second, we must note at the outset that none of the Western schemes of justice lays unequivocal claims to truth as the Islamic concept does. In this respect, perhaps the closest to Islam come certain strains in Greek philosophy, in particular Aristotelian thought. To the extent such systems focus on the essential nature or *telos* of humankind – which is equated with moral rationality – while elucidating the terms of participation in a political community, they strike a cord of harmony with the Islamic view of a human being and his/her purpose. In particular, if *telos* is unchanging, the basic rules of justice or social order too ought to remain constant. Truth in this sense is that which remains consistent, rather constant amidst the flow of things changing. This common position on the nature of humankind leads to some similarities in the profile of conduct required of individuals while dealing with others. On this account, one would think Christianity may also come close to Islamic thought. In fact, this was the case on matters of justice in exchange (i.e. the ban on usury) when the Church was in power. But since the Renaissance, the emphasis has been on the much quoted answer by Jesus on the question of taxes. Consider Matthew 22: v15-21 (Phillips edition):

> The Pharisees went off and discussed how they could trap him in argument. Eventually they sent their disciples with some of the Herod-party to say this, "Master, we know that you are an honest man who teaches the way of God faithfully and that you are not swayed by men's opinion of you. Obviously you don't care for human approval. Now tell us – Is it right to pay taxes to Caesar or not?"
>
> But Jesus knowing their evil intention said, "Why try this trick on me, you frauds? Show me the money you pay the tax with." They handed him a coin, and he said to them, "Whose face is this and whose name is in the inscription?"
>
> "Caesar's," they said.
>
> "Then give to Caesar," he replied, "what belongs to Caesar and to God what belongs to God!"

Focus on this Biblical injunction has encouraged a divergence in the West between the sacred and the secular. And as Junior (1993) observes, post Middle Ages, even the Church's teachings on issues such as usury, marriage, and religious freedom have undergone substantial change moving closer and closer to the accepted secular trends of the epoch, albeit with a lag. In Islam, however, separation between the realms of God and Caesar remains an anathema. In fact, the Qur'ān (5:46-7) goes a step further than this and interprets the mission of Jesus Christ (pbuh) (5:46-7) in no less equal terms. Why have these two civilizations then moved in opposite directions in understanding the very basic principles of running a society?

This brings us to the third observation on the differences between the two world-views, which stem from the different paths of their historical evolution. As Gellner (1981, p.2) points out, Christianity initially flourished among the politically disinherited and did not assume the role of Caesar for a considerable time. A potential for political modesty has, thus, stayed with it ever since. In comparison, Islam, unlike Christianity, was not born within an empire. On the contrary, Islam was born outside the two empires of its time and created an empire of its own that (closely identified, rather) found its legitimization in faith. Seen from a Muslim viewpoint then, Islam, acting as the blueprint as well as the social cement of a civilization, can neither be accused of corroding an earlier traditional civilization nor of living on as its ghost. It is only about Islam, therefore, that it can be said that all the good of that civilization can be attributed to motivation by faith and the bad to a deviation from the model set forth by the Prophet and his immediate successors. Analysts with European backgrounds tend to ignore this crucial difference when applying insights developed from studying Graeco-Roman history to Islamic civilization.

Fourth, and again alluding to the different paths of evolution of the two civilizations, Christianity, which began to take charge of the Roman Empire some two centuries prior to the rise of Islam, faced the trappings of a feudal system that albeit, not of its own making, as we saw above, was legitimized by it through resources outside the teachings of Christ (pbuh). Given that in the feudal society, most exchange was in kind, in line with Aristotelian ideas, Christianity retained for a considerable time an aversion to trading and market exchange. In contrast, Islam had had to deal with the problems associated with monetized free market exchange from its inception. Trading, as such, was extolled. What was considered necessary, however, was to elucidate what forms of exchange were unjust. On that account there is a detailed framework that prohibits usury, gambling and *gharar*, and even condemns unequal barter exchange encouraging instead monetized trade to avoid potential for uncertainty of value.

This brings us to the fifth point, the commonalities and differences between the modern Western views of justice and Islam. To begin with, one may argue that the lexicon of human rights is no stranger to Islam. Muslim scholars such as al- Ghazālī (1058-1111 CE) rationally interpreted the *Sharīʿah* as providing protection to one's religion, intellect, life, progeny and property. Nevertheless, unlike libertarianism, such rights were construed not as the absolutist starting point for defining a theory of justice but rather taken as signposts for the twin balancing of the private space *vis-à-vis* the public space and the private interest *vis-à-vis* the public interest. Once we move beyond this issue and examine finer details, we find that apart from the socialist concept of justice, other secular views are silent on the issue of just exchange. The Marxist (Soviet style) and libertarian views, for example, define two opposing poles. In the former, a planned economy, in any case has nothing akin to a market as we know it, i.e. the unhindered exchange of supply and demand signals through the price mechanism. In contrast to this is the libertarian view, which not only embraces the market in full but, in fact, takes the principles of 'negative freedoms' and 'Pareto optimality' that underlie a market exchange as benchmarks for measuring the achievements of the entire public sphere of a social order. Welfare liberalism, that attempts to strike a middle ground between these positions, too does not go very far from an Islamic perspective. Its focus remains on 'external', i.e. state sponsored correction of market outcomes through taxation and redistribution. To some extent this is complemented by an appreciation of the significance of workers' equity participation but this item has yet to be raised on the political agenda to the level *pari passu* with an emphasis on protecting the welfare system. The Islamic stand on this matter is that 'external' correction is needed to maintain the dignity of a 'fallen' human being, but on its own its reach could be too limited. It does not strike at the root of those mechanisms or exchanges 'internal' to the market that enable accumulation through means that are unfair and keep alive the possibility of *zulm* (oppression) on people by their own kind. Thus while the market itself is retained, the aim is to reform it 'internally' and organize it on a more dignified footing. It is perhaps this possibility that once prompted Musgrave (1985) to remind us that the equality of earnings from labour versus capital was never taken for granted by some renowned thinkers of the past. How come contemporary libertarians accept it without questioning? In fact, one can build further on this question and argue that there is a theoretical case for people pondering on terms of fair exchange, in particular from behind the Rawlsian veil of ignorance, to prefer a profit-and-loss sharing contract over a fixed interest contract as a more just basis of exchange. This issue assumes added importance when one considers that redistribution 'external' to the market is practised within certain national borders only, not outside them. In contrast, lending on fixed interest and continuous returns from it regardless of project outcomes continues to flow cross-border influencing the livelihood of the most poor in nations without the capacity to institute a welfare system.

Sixth, excepting modern libertarians,[19] there is a consensus among Christianity, Islam, socialist and welfare liberal concepts of justice on the need for redistribution. On this issue, Rawls' position and rationale that all differences among people are arbitrary from a moral perspective is in perfect harmony with Islam. Where Islam differs is on the solution. It first lays prime emphasis on the responsibility of individuals to fulfill their obligations to support their own selves, parents, family, neighbours, near relatives, and others. The idea is to keep those institutions and bonds intact that constitute the building blocks of a society, yet, make the state responsible for stepping in to assist in circumstances beyond an individual's control. Thus obligatory dues for redistribution – *zakāh* – may appear modest by some interpretations but its dedicated expenditure heads seek to prevent it from falling prey to the 'public choice' trappings of re-directing distribution away from the poor toward well off 'pressure groups' and lobbies. And, as we saw above, reforming market exchanges *per se* by banning usury and speculation complements such redistribution.

This brings us to the seventh and perhaps the most critical issue raised by some Western scholars, that of the incompatibility of religious traditions with democracy. The Islamic stand on this issue is very clear. The sacred books do not prohibit or recommend any specific method for the choice of government. This means that the modern 'procedure' of voting for electing a representative

---

[19]    John Locke is an exception. Consider, the following excerpt from his book: 'The right to the product of one's own labour does not permit one to let another person starve: God has given no one of his children such a property, in his peculiar portion of the things of this world, but that he has given his needy brother a right to the surplusage of his goods; so that it cannot justly be denied him, when his pressing wants call for it.' (Book 1, ch. 4, p.205). This third proviso seems to be a necessary consequence of Locke's basic idea that everyone must seek to preserve human life.' (cited in Sugden, 1992, p.280).

government is admissible. However, there are three caveats. First, the actions of government representatives, *pari passu* with the laity, must be subordinated strictly to the constitution. Second, the representatives' role as legislators ought to be circumscribed by the Islamic theory of justice. And, third, the elected government must be bound by a set of institutions – such as the judiciary and *ḥisbah* – that ensure accountability. This formulation ought not to trouble secular thinkers. For, as argued by Stepan (2000):

> Discursive traditions as dissimilar as the Enlightenment, liberalism, French republicanism, and modernization theory have all argued (or assumed) that modernity and democracy require secularism. From the viewpoint of empirical democratic practice, however, the concept of secularism must be radically rethought. At the very least, serious analysts must acknowledge ... that secularism and the separation of church and state have no inherent affinity with democracy, and indeed can be closely related to nondemocratic forms that systematically violate the twin tolerations.

Integrating the above elements into a vision for the role of the state in an economy, we find that insofar as Islam is concerned, the state enters into human life as a carrier and implementer of justice. Nowhere does Islam make it explicit that the market is the natural order that ought to serve as the benchmark for reflecting on or organizing other spheres of human interaction. Instead, market behaviour stands shoulder to shoulder with all other human interactions (that constitute socio-economic and political organization) ready to be examined and corrected with reference to the simple and complex goals of human life incorporated in the precepts of justice. Thus if freedom ought to be the goal, then processes as well as outcomes need to be geared toward this objective. When this consistency check – i.e. compatibility of goals versus process-cum-outcomes – is applied to the market, then Islam finds the need to prohibit certain forms of exchange and partially correct outcomes so as to close all gates to slavery. Again the comparison here is with Western philosophy (and standard economics based on it) that takes the market as the point of departure for defining the role of the state. Seen from this angle, there is a case for government intervention only in circumstances of market failure, i.e. imperfect competition, incomplete markets, and failure to reach competitive equilibrium. Thus, there is scope for regulating externalities (e.g. pollution), providing public goods (e.g. defence), alleviating moral hazard (through institutional means and legal enforcement), creating missing markets (e.g. compulsory third party insurance, student loans, etc.), fulfilling need (e.g. redistribution), and satisfying merit wants (e.g. schooling). The argument against entrusting some or many of these tasks to the public sector is based either on entitlement (i.e. the libertarian case against redistribution) or on the inability of the public sector to improve upon market outcomes. In other words, parallel to market failure are government failures; therefore, the former does not necessarily call for government action.

While there are similarities between the standard economic and Islamic perspectives, we believe an excessive emphasis of economics on the market as the benchmark and on tax-funded public goods as an alternative evades the potential of building upon and drawing out people's moral responsibility to correct market failure. Take, for example, the case of defence as a classical public good. It can be argued that by introducing the concept of *jihād*, i.e. personal moral responsibility to struggle against aggression, Islam leaves the door ajar for reducing paid armies[20] and instead focuses on the general preparatory training of every able-bodied person. At another level, it can be argued that an overemphasis on the public good argument has moved some developing countries onto the path of

---

[20]    From a public choice perspective, large armies may become an interest group on their own jeopardizing peace and public finance.

reckless debt financing of infrastructure that has definitely given access to their mineral resources but failed to generate equitable development or sufficient industrial progress so as to increase their ability to service the debt. By the time the infrastructure is due for an overhaul, budgets are still reeling with the debt burden and people – many having changed their lifestyles – can move into reverse gear. Thus there is the double pressure on governments of rising social tensions and squeezed margins to make fresh investments. One final point on this issue is that once we admit the claim that the market ought to be subjected to the tenets of justice, then the Islamic and the standard economic approaches to the role of the state are not necessarily mutually exclusive. There is great potential for both to learn from one another. How do these similarities and differences translate into the size of the public sector? Here, we introduce the following table from Kolm (1996):

**Table 1.3 : Philosophical commitment and the size of the public sector**

| Percent of GNP | Political Standpoint |
|---|---|
| 0 | Neo-libertarians |
| Low, decentralized, and diffused | Classical libertarians |
| 1 or 2% (plus army) | Minimal state (Locke-Nozick) |
| About 5% (plus army) | Hayek |
| About 8% (plus army) | M. Friedman |
| For example, 30% | Welfarist Public Economics |
| | Public Choice |
| For instance, 80% | Administrative socialism |

Adapted from Kolm, (1996, p.381).

What is the Islamic position? Naturally, it would vary from country to country depending on economic conditions. As a guess, if *zakāh* is estimated at some 5-7% of GNP, and on top of that one adds, say 8% plus for the army, then anything between 20-30% of GDP would sound a reasonable estimate provided that reforms internal to market exchange are carried out in accordance with the Islamic position on usury, gambling, and *gharar*. In the absence of such reforms, intuitively, greater wealth concentration is expected to continue and greater allocations for re-distribution 'external' to the market are expected to be required on a continuous basis.

This brings us to the last argument, that of the differences in the political ordering of the Islamic and the Western concepts of justice. Seen from one angle, the Islamic protection of the private space, its guarantee of not only the religious rites but also the personal laws of minorities, and its insistence on *Sharī'ah* law for the rest is equivalent to the Rawlsian position that there is a common political concept of the good but insofar as the private sphere of life, individuals are free to follow whatever concept they prefer.[21] However, there is one caveat. The Islamic permission to safeguard the personal law of each community provides a degree of freedom beyond the Rawlsian concept and is in essence aimed at keeping the metaphysical, through whatever tradition it is perceived, at the forefront of a person's life. In contrast, the modern secular visions of justice, by disallowing the freedom for individual traditions to observe different personal laws, gradually undermine the importance of the metaphysical in individual life. If this is correct, then some see a Pandora's box of issues unfolding or waiting in the wings. Tinder (1989) is typical:

---

[21]    Surely, Islam has many rules applicable to the private sphere, for example, marriage, separation, inheritance, food, prayers, festivals, etc. but these rules are applicable only to those who profess Islam.

many of the undoubted virtues of pluralism – respect for the individual and a belief in the essential equality of all human beings, to cite just two – have strong roots in the union of the spiritual and the political achieved in the vision of Christianity. The question that secularists have to answer is whether these values can survive without these particular roots. In short, can we be good without God? ... Today these values are honored more in the breach than in the observance ...' (p. 2 of 25)[22]

Lutz (2001) can also be taken to imply how tortuous it can become to employ the tools of rationality alone to justify even the fundamental tenet of an equitable social order – the equality of all human beings. It can be argued that if the implications of the theory of biological evolution are imported into this picture, the said tenet would in reality be reduced to a mere mantle piece. In comparison, Abrahamic religious traditions resolves this dilemma in one single statement, that of the origin of all men from Adam. In that lies the universal brotherhood of humankind with no real cause for a race for superiority and shedding the blood of one another. For sure, people of religion faltered in understanding the full demands of this principle but that reflects on them not on the principle *per se* that remains there to illuminate the path. The question that needs to be asked is where would it ultimately lead to, if the 'justification' of the very principle of equality is in doubt based on tools of rationality alone? Put another way, the major issue at stake, as we embark on the twenty-first century, is whether justice interpreted within the confines of maximizing the utility of dominant groups can survive the 'negative externalities' that it creates beyond these

---

22   Page numbers refer to the internet copy taken from: URL:<http:// theatlantic.com/election/connection/religion/goodgod.htm> (Access date 21/01/1999).

arbitrary boundaries. Note that this is not a matter of identity in which 'there is no sin' but rather a matter of guarding action that benefits self at the cost of others. And this latter principle is applicable as much to the comity of nations as it is to individuals because ultimately it is individuals who bear the brunt of 'negative externalities', whatever their source.

# Conclusions

We began this monograph by exploring what is justice? Our initial answer was: equality across some spheres of human action. If anything, contemporary libertarians are the closest in thought to this interpretation of justice. To them, equity means preservation of negative freedoms (full stop).[23] Beyond that, a positive call for the support of 'fallen' human beings is perceived as a requirement of charity but not of justice. This is because human beings are said to have the 'right' to own the usufruct of themselves. In challenging this right, many rival views on justice are at one, the Islamic concept being one of them, and in total agreement with the Rawlsian liberal welfare concept that all human inequalities are arbitrary from a moral standpoint. Yet, money makes the mare go, i.e. the role of incentives cannot be ignored. The two insights meet in admitting the market but supplementing its outcomes with state-sponsored support for the needy in order to protect human life and dignity. There are notable differences too between the welfare liberal and Islamic visions. First, the Islamic position is rooted in the

---

[23] In taking this stand, they strike a cord of harmony with the concept of justice that prevailed in pre-Islamic Arabia.

metaphysical concept that the present life is a test regarding whether one fulfils responsibilities as the trustee of God on earth. The nature of these responsibilities means that the challenge lies not in freeing oneself for what Aristotle calls the pursuit of the highest good – contemplation of unchanging truths *per se* – but rather in using such soul-searching as a means to internalizing universal moral truths so as to undermine inhibitions within a person (e.g., pride, greed) that compel one to indulge in injustice and miserliness. With that reformed frame of mind, justice and benevolence flow naturally and so does socio-political action to universalize these attributes. Second, while encouraging redistribution, there is a great encouragement in Islam on preserving the social structure, in particular that of family. Thus justice and charity begin at home. To this end, there are mutual rights and obligations among parents, children and near kin, and there is obligatory distribution of inheritance among the extended family. And finally, Islam goes a step further than redistribution 'external' to the market and family architecture. It calls for reforming those market exchanges – those constitute the basis of entitlement to earnings – that it considers inherently oppressive, i.e. usury, speculation, and *gharar*, thus, providing the basis for the diffusion of human success across all spectrums of population through cooperative rather than conflict based modes of financial and business interaction. This is tantamount to the Islamic way of 'civilizing global capital', a topic that has attracted many writers in the West over the last two decades. With these differences, and against the backdrop of admitting intrinsic brotherhood among all human beings and the hierarchical protection of religion, life, honour, family, and property, it can be safely assumed that in its overall structure, the Islamic concept of justice appears much closer to a moral polyarchy geared toward the empowerment and spiritual, moral and material enrichment of human beings at large. The idea is to satisfy existing needs as well as fashion future wants in a manner that upholds justice, protects fundamental social institutions, promotes solidarity, and advances peace. Above all, it is to please the Almighty God Who has created human beings to serve one another so as to serve Him.

# Bibliography

1. Ashtor, E. 1976. *A Social and Economic History of the Near East in the Middle Ages*. London: Collins.
2. Beauchamp, T. L. and Norman Bowie (eds.). 2001. *Ethical Theory and Business*. New Jersey: Prentice Hall.
3. Bentham, Jerry. 1789. *Principles of morals and legislation*. Edited by J. Bowring, *The Internet Encyclopedia of Philosophy*. 22 Jan 2002: http://www.utm.edu:80/research/iep/text/bentham/benthpri.htm.
4. Bhutto, Zulfikar Ali. 1976. 'World Muslim Unity: Address to the Islamic Summit held in Lahore, 22 February 1974'. In *Thoughts on Some Aspects of Islam*. Lahore: Sh. Muhammad Ashraf.
5. Bowle, John. 1961. *Western Political Thought*. London: Methuen & Co. Ltd.
6. Chapra, M. Umer. 1992. *Islam and the Economic Challenge*. Leicester, UK: The Islamic Foundation.
7. Dworkin, Ronald. 1981. 'What is Equality? Part 2: Equality of Resources'. *Philosophy and Public Affairs* 10 (4): 283-345.
8. El-Awa, Mohamed S. 1983. *Punishment in Islamic Law: A Comparative Study*. Delhi: Markazi Maktaba Islami.
9. Esposito, John L. 1995. *The Islamic Threat: Myth or Reality?* New York, Oxford: Oxford University Press.

10. Fusfeld, Daniel R. 1999. *The Age of the Economist*. 8th ed. Massachusetts: Addison-Wesley.

11. Gellner, Ernest. 1981. *Muslim society*. Cambridge: Cambridge University Press.

12. Gellner, Ernest. 1992. *Postmodernism, Reason and Religion*. London, New York: Routledge.

13. Ḥadīth: Most *Aḥādīth* quoted in the thesis are taken from the relevant books stored in The Alim for Windows Release 4.5 (1986). ISL Software Corporation, USA and Canada.

14. Harmon, M. Judd. 1964. *Political Thought from Pluto to the Present*. New York: McGraw-Hill Book Company.

15. Haslett, David W. 1994. *Capitalism with Morality*. New York: Oxford University Press.

16. Hausman, Daniel M. and McPherson, Michael S. 1996. *Economic Analysis and Moral Philosophy*. Cambridge, UK: Cambridge University Press.

17. Hayek, F. A. 1976. *Law, Legislation and Liberty: Volume 2 The Mirage of Social Justice*. Chicago: University of Chicago Press.

18. Heilbroner, Robert L. 1967. *The Worldly Philosophers*. 3rd revised ed. New York: Simon & Schuster.

19. Hitti, Philip K. 1970. *History of the Arabs*. 11th reprint, 1986 ed. London: Macmillan Education Ltd., Macmillan International College Editions.

20. Hoffe, Otfried. 1995. *Political Justice*. Translated by J. C. Cohen. Cambridge, UK: Polity Press.

21. Holcombe, Randall G. 1998. 'The Foundations of Normative Public Finance'. In *Handbook of Public Finance*, edited by F. Thompson and M. T. Green. New York: Marcel Dekker, Inc.

22. *The Holy Qur'ān: English Translation of the Meanings and Commentary*, trans. Allama Abdullah Yusuf Ali, ed. The Presidency of Islamic Researches, *Ifta*, Call and Guidance.

Al-Madinah Al-Munawwarah: King Fahd Holy Qur'an Printing Complex.

23. Iqbal, Justice Javid. 1986. 'The Concept of State in Islam'. In *State, Politics, and Islam,* edited by M. Ahmad. Indianapolis: American Trust Publications.

24. Junior, John T. Noonan. 1993. 'Development in Moral Doctrine'. *Theological Studies* 54 (4): 662(16).

25. Kolm, Serge-Christophe. 1996. *Modern Theories of Justice.* Cambridge, Massachusetts: The MIT Press.

26. Kramnick, Issac, ed. 1969. *Essays in the History of Political Thought.* New Jersey: Prentice Hall.

27. Lewis, Bernard. 1993. 'Islam and Liberal Democracy'. *The Atlantic* 271 (2): 89-98.

28. Lutz, Mark A. 2001. 'On the norm of equality'. *International Journal of Social Economics* 28 (10, 11, 12): 782-799.

29. MacIntyre, Alasdair. 1966. *A Short History of Ethics.* London: Routledge & Kegan Paul.

30. MacIntyre, Alasdair. 1985. *After Virtue.* Second (corrected) ed. London: Gerald Duckworth & Co. Ltd.

31. Maudūdī, S. Abul A'lā. 1994. *Economic System of Islam.* Translated by Riaz Husain. Edited by K. Ahmad. 2nd ed. Lahore: Islamic Publications Ltd.

32. Miller, David, ed. 1991. *The Blackwell Encyclopaedia of Political Thought.* Oxford: Blackwell Publishers.

33. Muller, Jerry Z. 1993. *Adam Smith in his Time and Ours: Designing the Decent Society.* New York: The Free Press (A Division of Macmillan, Inc.).

34. Musgrave, Richard A. 1959. *The Theory of Public Finance.* New York: McGraw-Hill Book Company.

35. Musgrave, Richard A. 1985. 'Public Finance and Distributive Justice'. In *Public Choice, Public Finance and Public Policy,* edited by D. Greenaway and G. K. Shaw. Oxford, UK: Basil Blackwell Ltd.

36. Nozick, R. 1974. *Anarchy, State and Utopia*. New York: Basic Books.
37. Pigou, A. C. 1918. *The Economics of Welfare*. London: Macmillan.
38. Rawls, John. 1971. *A Theory of Justice*. Cambridge, Massachusetts: The Belknap Press of Harvard University Press.
39. Robbins, L. 1935. *Nature and Significance of Economic Science*, London: Macmillan.
40. Robinson, Francis. 1996. 'Introduction'. In *Islamic World*, edited by Robinson, Francis, Cambridge: Cambridge University Press: xi-xxiii.
41. Rowley, C. K., ed. 1993. *Social Choice Theory*. Aldershot, Hants: Edward Elgar Publishing Limited.
42. Sen, Amartya. 1985. 'Well-being, Agency and Freedom: The Dewey Lectures'. *The Journal of Philosophy* 82 (4): 169-221.
43. Sen, Amartya. 1987. *On Ethics and Economics*. Oxford: Basil Blackwell Ltd.
44. Sen, Amartya. 1992. *Inequality Re-examined*. Oxford: Oxford University Press.
45. Sen, Amartya. 1993. 'Markets and Freedoms: Achievements and Limitations of the Market Mechanism in Promoting Individual Freedoms'. *Oxford Economic Papers* 45: 519-541.
46. Sen, Amartya. 1999. *Development as Freedom*. New York: Knopf.
47. Siddiqi, M. Nejatullah. 1996. *Role of the State in the Economy*. Leicester, UK: The Islamic Foundation.
48. Smirnov, A. 1996. 'Understanding Justice in an Islamic Context: Some Points of Contrast With Western Theories'. *Philosophy East and West* 46 (3): 337(14).
49. Smith, Adam. [1776] 1966. *The Wealth of Nations*. Edited by E. A. Seligman. 2 vols. Vol. 2. London: J. M. Dent & Sons Ltd., Everyman's Library.
50. Spiegel, Henry William. 1971. *The Growth of Economic Thought*. Englewood Cliffs, New Jersey: Prentice-Hall, Inc.

51. Stepan, Alfred. 2000. 'Religion, Democracy, and the "Twin Tolerations"'. *Journal of Democracy* 11 (4): 37-57.
52. Sterba, James P. 1992. 'Introduction'. In *Justice: Alternative Political Perspectives*. Belmont, California: Wadsworth Publications.
53. Stiglitz, Joseph E. 1994. *Whither Socialism?* Massachusetts: The MIT Press.
54. Sugden, Robert. 1992. 'Social Justice'. In *The Theory of Choice: A Critical Guide*, edited by Shaun Hargreaves et al. Oxford, UK: Blackwell Publishers.
55. Tahir-ul-Qadri, Dr. Muhammad. 1995. *Islamic Philosophy of Human Life*. Lahore: Minhaj-ul-Quran Publications.
56. 'The Nature of Justice (A chapter translated from *Nichomachean Ethics)'*. 1992. In *Justice: Alternative Political Perspectives*, edited by J. P. Sterba. Belmont, California: Wadsworth Publications: 207-18.
57. Tinder, Glenn. 1989. 'Can We Be Good Without God?' *Atlantic Monthly* 264 (6):69-85.
58. Usher, Dan. 1992. *The Welfare Economics of Markets, Voting and Predation*. Manchester: Manchester University Press.
59. Wells, H. G. 1961. *The Outline of History*. London: Cassell & Company Ltd.
60. Zarqa, Dr. Anas. 1980. 'Islamic Economics: An Approach to Human Welfare'. In *Studies in Islamic Economics*, edited by K. Ahmad. Leicester, UK: The Islamic Foundation.